'There are many tales of Scottish m
inspiration to read this account of
to Jesus Christ, lived out with cour
China's turbulent periods. This sto
humble beginnings in Greenock should encourage us all to be confident in the gospel and in God's power.'

*Elaine Duncan, Chief Executive, Scottish Bible Society*

'A remarkable story and man! A Glasgow-trained doctor and missionary who battled against huge odds to establish the first Western medical school in Imperial China, set in the heart of Peking.'

*Sir Kenneth Calman, Chancellor of the University of Glasgow*

'Andrew has skilfully researched previously inaccessible material on Thomas Cochrane, deepening our understanding of this fascinating man and his extraordinary achievements, and of the crucial role played by his devoted wife Grace.'

*Thomas Cochrane FRCS(Ed), retired consultant surgeon*
*and grandson of Dr T. J. Cochrane*

'Quite a few years ago, a Western scholar claimed that British missionaries, coming mainly from the lower classes, went to China in anticipation of a higher standard of living.

Andrew Adam's informative biography of the medical missionary Thomas Cochrane quickly disabuses readers of that idea. He vividly portrays the doctor's compassionate work in primitive and even precarious conditions immediately following his arrival in north China's hinterland on the eve of the violently anti-foreign Boxer Uprising. The benevolent interventions of this remarkable Scotsman continued during the first decade of the twentieth century. By effectively appealing to the powers that be, Dr Cochrane succeeded in improving public health standards, thereby preventing the worst effects of a cholera epidemic that had spread to Peking.

The most fascinating section of the book concerns the unexpected encounters of the erstwhile "foreign devil" with the imperial eunuch Li Lianying and the Empress Dowager Cixi. The well-told story of

Thomas Cochrane's stubborn commitment to serve the ordinary people of China while relentlessly promoting the missionary cause makes this book a wonderfully engaging read.'

*R. G. Tiedemann, Professor of Modern Chinese History,*
*Shandong University, Jinan, China*

Andrew Adam was born in London in 1939 into a medical family. Torn between the family tradition and the humanities, he read history at Merton College Oxford, then worked as a journalist on *The Times*, before switching to medicine. He paid his way through medical school – while supporting a wife and child – by freelance journalism and male modelling, a cocktail which baffled his tutors.

He spent 16 years in the Royal Air Force as a medical officer where he took further training as a pathologist and gained expertise in fatal aircraft crash investigations. He also served at the US Armed Forces Institute of Pathology in Washington DC. All the while, the writing continued: a stream of fiction, essays and historical pieces, most of them published under pseudonyms. Senior RAF officers of that era cast a baleful eye on junior officers with literary intentions.

In 1983 he left the service to become a hospital consultant in Somerset. Since retiring from medicine he has been a church elder, a police chaplain, a street pastor, the chairman of an evangelistic trust and the facilitator of a movement for church unity. He is a guest speaker on Cunard liners, a role which takes him and his wife around the world. The rest of his time is happily filled with their three children and six grandchildren, and with writing.

In the margin of his diaries Andrew's step-grandfather, Thomas Cochrane, frequently wrote the word *Excelsior*. It is Latin for 'Upwards!' Andrew likes that. 'For those who follow Jesus,' he says, 'there's always a horizon beyond the one you can see.'

*Dr Thomas J. Cochrane (1866–1953)*
Cochrane Family Collection

# THOMAS COCHRANE AND THE DRAGON THRONE

*Confronting disease, distrust and murderous rebellion in Imperial China*

Andrew E. Adam

First published in Great Britain in 2018

Society for Promoting Christian Knowledge
36 Causton Street
London SW1P 4ST
www.spck.org.uk

*British Library Cataloguing-in-Publication Data*
A catalogue record for this book is available from the British Library

ISBN 978–0–281–08036–6
eBook ISBN 978–0–281–08037–3

Typeset by Geethik, India
First printed in Great Britain by Jellyfish Print Solutions
Subsequently digitally reprinted in Great Britain

eBook by Geethik, India

Produced on paper from sustainable forests

*To my wife Jacqui, who has always believed in me. She has been my encourager, keel and stabilizer in every situation*

# Contents

# Contents

# Illustrations

## List of illustrations

# *Preface*

Between 1850 and 1950 approximately 1,500 doctors left Britain to serve as medical missionaries around the world. With the exception of those who were also explorers like David Livingstone or scientists like Patrick Manson, their names are largely forgotten.

These doctors and the nurses who accompanied them worked in arduous conditions. They were at the mercy of the diseases they treated and they paid a high price in health and early death. They faced isolation, homesickness, nervous breakdowns and suicide. They were reviled by the people they tried to help, and sometimes their own missionary societies failed to appreciate them; for decades a man with a stethoscope was valued far below a man in a dog collar.

One of the hardest places on earth for a medical missionary was China. Its people had a huge sense of cultural superiority and clung to their traditions in medicine and pharmacy. After decades of being exploited by the 'foreign devils', they hated the missionaries almost as much as the merchants. Christianity seemed to threaten everything that the Chinese held dear. When Tom Cochrane and his bride arrived in 1897 in China's northernmost region, the land was like Jeremiah's boiling pot, spilling over from the north.

Over 30 years ago my mother, Margaret Aitchison, who was Tom's stepdaughter, wrote an account of his early life entitled *The Doctor and the Dragon*. He had intended to write a book himself and his papers include drafts which never saw printer's ink. She began writing in 1966, the year of the Cultural Revolution, when she was living in the Canary Isles. The practical difficulties proved too great, but she resumed the task a decade later when in her seventies, thumping away on an old manual typewriter. She struggled through a heart attack and shingles and she had no Internet to help her. I admire her achievement, but am conscious of its limitations.

Today China is a superpower moving rapidly towards the centre of the world stage. Interest in the nation's past is growing and we need to understand what it has come through. We need also to admit that Britain's conduct in the nineteenth century did the Chinese people great harm and to hang our heads. That is the universal view in China and it is taught in its classrooms. But equally we should not forget the good work that missionaries, doctors, educationalists, philanthropists and entrepreneurs did in China, often at great personal cost. That is one reason for writing this book.

I have used Tom Cochrane's papers to tell his story from a different perspective, that of a medical doctor who as a boy knew him well. I believe my mother would have approved, because we both loved and admired 'the Doc'. He was a hero of the Christian faith whose achievements deserve to be remembered.

***

Note: Throughout the book I have used Romanized place names. My generation is more comfortable with Peking than Beijing, Canton than Guangzhou, and Mukden than Shenyang. If this seems retrograde to Chinese readers, I apologize and plead no disrespect. The Empress Dowager is an exception. Cixi (pronounced *tseshee*) is more memorable and easier to spell than Tzu-Hsi or Tsu-Hsi.

# Acknowledgements

Every biography has its prompters and midwives. This one was first prompted by my mother, Margaret Aitchison, whose account of her stepfather's life in China appeared a generation ago. It left me intrigued but unsatisfied, as did Francesca French's official biography which dates back to 1956. Both books considered Thomas Cochrane primarily as a missionary and focused on his spiritual life but were short on hard facts. As a doctor I wanted to know how he and other medical missionaries managed to survived professionally in the harshest of conditions, let alone dream great dreams and achieve them.

On my mother's death in 1988 I inherited a boxful of Thomas Cochrane's papers. For further background information I am indebted to the School of Oriental and African Studies (SOAS) in London. It owns the largest collection of missionary papers in the UK, including the archives of the London Missionary Society, and its library staff proved both knowledgeable and helpful. The Archive Services at Glasgow University supplied details of Tom's medical education. John Burleigh, a native of Greenock and a Cochrane enthusiast, also helped. I suspect that he will not rest until Inverclyde Council produces a commemorative blue plaque.

I am especially grateful to Gary Tiedemann, professor of Chinese history at Shandong University, Jinan, and a research associate at SOAS. His area of special interest embraces missionaries and Christianity in northern China between 1800 and 1949 so his expertise is unique. His advice on an early draft saved me from a variety of possible errors. Any that persist are entirely my own doing.

I am also indebted to Professor Norman Kutcher of the history faculty at Syracuse University, New York, for details of the titles and roles of the imperial eunuchs.

Thomas D. Cochrane is a distinguished plastic surgeon (now retired) and the fourth generation to bear the name. He has provided invaluable help with information about his grandfather as well as allowing me the run of his collection of photographs and papers. Marion Cochrane, daughter-in-law and biographer of Robert Cochrane, also helped with family reminiscences.

As for midwives, Ali Hull is the critic and coach every writer needs: dispassionate, razor sharp and unfailingly constructive. I have known her for years and she taught me the principles of biography writing. Her enthusiasm, backed up by scores of emails, kept me at the task. So has the support of my generous-hearted wife Jacqui and other family members.

Ali Hull also found the publishers for the book, which brings me finally to the team at SPCK. Tony Collins and I both started life as journalists in the days of curled-up galley proofs which were six feet long. You chopped them to size with tailor's scissors, dropped in illustrations and captions, and stuck everything on a template with a foul-smelling substance called cow gum.

My understanding of the publishing process had advanced little from those days, so besides overseeing the book's production Tony has midwifed me in the new technology. My thanks also go to Dr Rima Devereaux and to Mollie Barker for dealing expertly and sympathetically with the text.

I thank Sir Kenneth Calman, Mr Thomas D. Cochrane, Professor Gary Tiedemann and Ms Elaine Duncan for reading and endorsing the book.

# A note on the Boxer Uprising of 1900

Most people today know nothing about the Boxer Uprising, which was the greatest disaster in missionary history. Later atrocities have eclipsed the events that took place in 1900 on the other side of the world. The last time the Boxers were in the public eye was in 1963, when Samuel Bronston's lacklustre movie *Fifty-five Days at Peking* was released. Few remember it now or remembered the Boxers' victims in their centennial year.

The uprising has a pivotal place in Tom Cochrane's story, so I give an outline here. It arose out of China's grievances against the West which came to a head in the last days of the Manchu or Qing dynasty (1644–1912). The Manchus were usurpers from Manchuria and formed only a tenth of the population. They were hated by the Chinese, and they ruled by fear and force.

Historians point to the disastrous war with Japan in 1894 as a major cause of the Boxer Uprising and the death knell of the Chinese Empire. But a more immediate trigger was a series of natural disasters in the late 1890s. Widespread drought alternated with the severe flooding of China's two main waterways, the Yellow River and the Yangtze River. Millions died as one harvest after another failed or was washed away. The price of grain rocketed and famine broke out. The Imperial Government could do little to help and the starving peasants were soon radicalized.

They were led by a powerful secret society called the Yihequan, or 'Fists United in Harmony', whose members were devoted to the martial arts; for that reason they were dubbed 'Boxers' by the foreign press.[1] Many were in their teens but, like today's child soldiers, when

---

[1] The evolution of the Boxer movement is more complicated than often stated. An early element emerged in Chihli province and was known as the 'Plum Flower Boxers'. By 1898 they had changed their name to 'Fists United in Harmony'. In late 1898 a separate element emerged in north-west Shantung province, known as the 'Spirit Boxers'. When dislodged by imperial troops, they moved into Chihli and joined forces there. I am indebted to the research of Professor Gary Tiedemann.

indoctrinated they were capable of the most terrible atrocities. They practised secret rites, incantations, trances and ecstatic fits. They had no uniforms and wore scarlet shirts and scarves with a variety of headgear.

The Boxers were a shadowy bunch with no hierarchy or supreme commander and, like most peasant movements, they left no written records. Convinced that their martial exercises and charms protected them from bullets, they scorned firearms and preferred swords and long-handled poles with axe heads. This cost them dearly in the street fighting in Peking.

They were violently hostile towards the foreigners whom they blamed for China's misfortunes. Most foreigners lived in the treaty ports, protected by European troops and gunships. But hundreds of missionaries lived in China's interior, sharing their lives with the common people. Some were women, working alone or in pairs. Like the Cochranes in Inner Mongolia, they were defenceless, as were tens of thousands of converts.

In 1899 the Boxers roamed the northern provinces in bands, destroying churches, schools, orphanages, dispensaries, hospitals, bookstores and homes. They burned them to the ground and scattered the bricks so that no traces remained. Around Peking and Tientsin they ripped up railway tracks and tore down telegraph wires. They intimidated the local officials, and in some towns the mandarins were forced to incorporate them into the local militias.

The Imperial Government's response was to declare the Boxers illegal and try to disperse them, but that was not enough for the Great Powers. As the famine deepened and violence spread, an ultimatum went out in April 1900 to the Chinese government. The message was clear: 'Exterminate the Boxers within two months or take the consequences.'[2]

The Empress Dowager Cixi, the ruler of China, had a dilemma. Personally she was displeased by the violence and the potential damage to her policies, but she knew the Boxers' popularity and her lack of it. She was loath to kill large numbers of them in case they rallied and turned on the monarchy. But she also had to placate the Great Powers

---

[2] These nations all had sizable trading interests in China. They were Britain, France, Germany, Russia, Austro-Hungary, Italy, the USA and Japan.

and avoid a punitive expedition which could bring down the Manchu regime. She walked a tightrope, condemning the Boxers publicly while supporting them secretly.

By June 1900 the famine had brought 200,000 half-starved rebels to the capital, where they outnumbered the imperial troops. The streets were awash with scarlet sashes and seethed with discontent. Cixi tried to limit the damage to European property while at the same time permitting the Boxers to link up with the regulars and to draw weapons from the imperial armoury. On 21 June she threw in her lot with the Boxers and declared war on the Eight Nations. It was tantamount to declaring war on the whole world. Fortunately the refusal of certain courageous provincial governors to obey the order prevented an even greater disaster from occurring.

There followed the famous Siege of the Legations. The attention of the civilized world was focused on one small spot in Peking, the British legation and its surroundings. Here the defenders held off an army of fanatics set on exterminating them. Their families in Europe endured an agonizing silence because the telegraph lines were cut and no information got out.[3] After eight weeks a column of allied troops fought its way up from the coast, broke the siege and fell on the city like crusaders entering Jerusalem.

At the last moment, Cixi escaped from Peking disguised as a peasant, with her nephew, the Emperor Guangxu. They fled to Xian in Shanxi province. There they stayed until January 1902, by which time it was safe to return and make amends.

The Boxer Protocol which followed was largely dictated by the Eight Nations of the military alliance, supported by Belgium, Spain and the Netherlands. It demanded massive financial compensation from China. Cixi was allowed to resume the government so that she could maintain order and collect the taxes that would pay for the compensation. Thus she narrowly held on to the throne.

The events of 1900 are sometimes called a rebellion rather than an uprising, probably because rebellions were frequent events in nineteenth-

---

[3] The British were getting used to lengthy sieges, thanks to the Second Boer War. The siege of Kimberley (which lasted 124 days) finished in February 1900 and Mafeking (217 days) finished in May. The siege of Ladysmith (118 days) began in November 1900.

century China. But the Boxers' aim was to expel the foreigners and exterminate everything Christian, rather than to overthrow the Manchus, or conversely to restore the Emperor, whom Cixi had deposed two years earlier. They made no serious attack on imperial troops and in Peking fought alongside them. The label of 'rebellion' seems to have originated with the Great Powers to save the face of the Empress Dowager, whose perfidious regime they were obliged to support. The term 'uprising' therefore seems to me more accurate.

Whatever their individual motives, the Boxers exacted a terrible vengeance. Over 30,000 Chinese Christians and 239 missionaries were butchered. Tom Cochrane and his family were among those who survived.

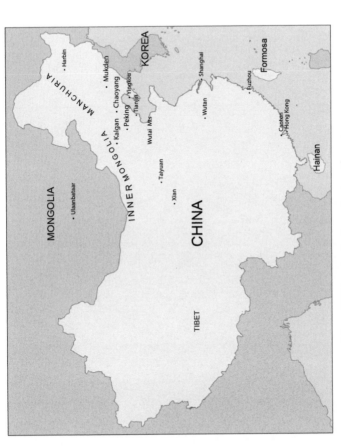

*Map of China in the late nineteenth century*

# 1

## *Journey to the interior*

*A seagoing junk of the 1890s like the one in which Tom and Grace travelled*

An Underwood & Underwood stereophoto. Library of Congress, Prints & Photographs Division

Around a jetty in the remote seaport of Yingkou in north-eastern China the tide was rising fast. Here the Yellow Sea narrows into the Gulf of Bohai and the waters are shallow and treacherous. Masts and broken spars rose above the waves, marking where junks had come to grief. The tide slapped rhythmically against the wooden piles, creating drifts of spume where recently there had been ice.

It was a cold blustery day in April 1897 and people scurried about their business. Gangs of coolies were loading crates of linseed while Russian traders in Cossack trousers argued over bales of furs. Drunken ratings searched for their ship and Manchurian bannermen in quilted coats were returning from an archery contest. The families that worked the commercial junks also lived on them and kept chickens and pigs on board; the air reeked of fish, hot oil and animals.

A young couple standing on the jetty stood out as new arrivals. She shivered in an English-made overcoat, while he wore a Manchurian cap with earflaps which ill-matched his suit and brogues. Physically they made an interesting contrast. Tom Cochrane was a 30-year-old Scot from Greenock, short and stocky with dark hair, a strong jaw and a bristling moustache. He was light on his feet and gentle in his ways, but his piercing grey eyes and impatient manner declared he was a man with a purpose. People often found his steely gaze unnerving, but there was nothing unkind about it. He watched the comings and goings on the jetty with what seemed to be an experienced eye.

His wife Grace was also Scottish. She was dark-haired and slender, a little taller than her husband, and she had a natural Celtic charm. As a gale whistled through the masts, she held tightly to his arm, suspecting from the glances she received that this was not etiquette. She was right. In China a respectable woman did not parade at her husband's side; she stayed in her house.

They had come by steamship from Southampton to Shanghai, a voyage of 12,000 miles that took six weeks. When they reached Shanghai, the port of Tientsin (modern Tianjin) was frozen, so they waited until shipping broke through the ice. They planned to do the last stage of their journey overland, but were advised to take another steamer across the Gulf of Bohai to Yingkou. There they would find a junk for the dead-leg back to the western shore. This would reduce the length of the overland journey and would be safer, or so they were told.

Also on the jetty was the Revd John Parker (1861–1944), a missionary of the London Missionary Society who had met them in Tientsin. Five years older than Tom, he had several years' experience of north China and the town where they were headed. Without him they would have been helpless. The previous evening he had selected one filthy junk out of a hundred and haggled in a smoke-filled cabin with the crew.

The 35-foot junk lay among a tangle of junks and sampans along the ramshackle jetty. To Tom's eye the vessel looked fitter for firewood than a sea voyage. Two glaring eyes were painted on the bows and a fringe of seaweed flowed around the stern. Its sails were mottled with age.

There was a commotion on board as the barefoot crew chased a cockerel round the deck and decapitated it before their eyes. They dribbled its blood into the sea with much prostrating and chanting. John Parker said there was no cause for concern; it was a routine precaution. A sacrifice to the ship's goddess to protect against ship-wreck . . .

One of the crew shouldered their cases. The Cochranes were about to receive their first lesson in oriental endurance. The voyage of 70 miles that was supposed to take 12 hours would turn into a nightmare lasting six days.

Their cabin was a slit-like compartment, measuring five feet by eight feet, which they entered by sliding down a plank through a hatch. It was so small they could barely stand upright on the floor, which was covered with twigs and straw. Grace thought it was more like a coffin than a cabin. After a few hours at sea Tom agreed with her; it seemed likely to become their final resting place.

That night they lay on a bamboo mat, pressed so closely together that if one of them wanted to turn over, they both had to do so. Once they were at sea, the crew covered the hatch and they lay in darkness listening to the waves crashing against the hull. A storm forced them to shelter in a creek, within sight of a village which had a sinister repu-tation. Piracy was rife in those seas, with small fast junks preying upon larger commercial ones. Sure enough, when they put to sea again, pir-ates pursued and made a determined attempt to overhaul them. The crew frantically put on more sail and they were able to draw away.

For most of the time the Cochranes kept to the cabin. They could not change their clothes and 'China's millions' made sleep impossible. These were the bedbugs that teemed in the straw and sucked their blood.

On the fifth day the food and water ran out. The sixth day was a prayer day and the crew burned joss sticks on the deck. Tom got on his hands and knees so that Grace could climb onto his back and scram-ble up the plank. He scanned the coast, seasick and not in the best of spirits. Later he wrote, 'If there was any romantic element in my decision to become a medical missionary, it vanished as I gazed disconsolately at the muddy shores of Manchuria and realised that as a foreigner there was no welcome for me there.'

\*\*\*

The irony was that Tom had never planned to go to China. Circumstances had directed it, like a storm that forces a ship on to a new course. Tom was born in the port of Greenock on the River Clyde in 1866, the eldest child of Thomas and Catherine Cochrane. His father described himself in documents as a clerk or porter. He earned a meagre living selling groceries to ships in Greenock docks.

Greenock is 30 miles downstream from Glasgow, and from its quays and docks ships sailed all over the world. It was a tough salty community with many taverns and a reputation for hard drinking. But although the town council conducted its business in taprooms, many Greenock folk were rigid Calvinists. Some of this undoubtedly rubbed off on Tom, who abominated tobacco and never touched hard drink. His parents were Congregationalists and his father wanted him to study theology and enter the ministry.

As a youngster Tom loved learning and was usually top of his class. He came to faith at the age of eight, when the American evangelist D. L. Moody ran a crusade in Glasgow and preached in a hall in Greenock in the spring of 1874. Ira Sankey sang a revivalist hymn and the boy felt the thrill of the words:

> Too late, too late will be the cry.
> Jesus of Nazareth has just passed by!

Then Moody walked to the front of the platform and spoke without an introduction. 'There may be someone here who is repeating the verse, "Believe in the Lord Jesus Christ and you will be saved", but he's wondering what *to believe* means.' It seemed to Tom that Moody was addressing him personally because the question had haunted him for days. That night he became a Christian.

On 4 March 1880 his father died at the age of 37, leaving the family penniless. As so often happened in Victorian working-class families,

Tom's childhood ended abruptly. Within a week he was working ten hours a day in a sugar broker's office for a salary of £10 a year. In the evenings he helped his mother to carry on the family business. It was tough work, balancing heavy baskets of provisions up ships' gangways, avoiding buckets and ropes.

The next few years were marked by hardships which gave an edge to Tom's character. It showed in various ways: his thrift and hatred of waste, his self-discipline and capacity for hard work, and his dogged refusal to accept failure. His sense of duty showed clearly when he took responsibility for his brother, sister and mother. Throughout his teens he was their provider and protector.

Catherine Cochrane was a great encourager and she constantly urged her children to make the best of their opportunities. In his late teens Tom underwent a spiritual awakening, caused partly by reading *Decision of Character* written by the Evangelical writer John Foster. It put his mind in a whirl and he started to study for the civil service examinations. Later his thoughts turned to the overseas mission field. When he learned of the opportunities open to *medical* missionaries, he was relieved because preparing three sermons a week seemed beyond him. He would rather practise his faith than preach it, and from then onwards he was set on becoming a doctor.

A medical degree must have seemed wishful thinking when every penny he earned went on feeding his family. Nevertheless Tom decided to take the preliminary examination for Glasgow University. He went at the challenge like a terrier, and when he joined a night class for chemistry, he came top out of 50 students. The university examiners were impressed; if this young man could scrape together £100 for the fees and a pound a week for his board and lodging, they would take him.

He wrote, 'How I did it I don't know. I neither had good food nor good health nor proper exercise, but I managed on a total of about three hundred and fifty pounds.' A bargain price for a medical degree! It gives an idea of Tom's capacity for discipline and restraint.

While he was at medical school, he read some words written by General Charles George Gordon, who had been killed a few years earlier in the Sudan and was regarded in some quarters as a martyr. He copied them into the flyleaf of his Bible:

> There is not the least doubt that there is an immense virgin field for an apostle in these countries among the black tribes but where will they find an apostle? A man must give up everything, understand everything, everything! He must be dead to the world, have no ties of any sort and long for death when it may please God to take him. There are few, very few such and yet what a field!

From then on, whenever Tom thought of the mission field, it was the Sudan. He wrote, 'I thought that region was the neediest on earth.'

In the event he approached the London Missionary Society. It was interdenominational in ethos and Congregational in its membership, both of which fitted his background. The Society was founded in 1795 with a vision 'to spread the knowledge of Christ among heathen and other unenlightened nations'. Its better-known servants included Robert Moffat and David Livingstone in Africa, John Adam in India, and Robert Morrison who was the first Protestant missionary to mainland China.

At an appointments meeting in the Society's headquarters in 1896, his interviewers were intrigued to learn that Tom had left school at 13. What happened to his education? Tom guessed they were wondering how he had scraped into medical school without formal schooling. He told them about the evening classes, the librarian who obtained books for him, the family doctor who tutored him, and the support of his minister and church. He had burned gallons of midnight oil before he entered Glasgow Medical School in 1892 at the age of 26.

It was a thorough probing. They had to know he was made of the right stuff; a wrong decision could cost lives. Was he sound in faith and doctrine? Was he physically strong? Was he practical with his hands? Was he really an *evangelist*? (It was folly to send a medical man simply because he was an evangelist and madness to send him if he were not.)

Tom spoke slowly when careful answers were called for. An evangelist? He had made his first convert a few days after he became a Christian. It was a boy his own age. From then on he did his best to win a soul a week.

The board members exchanged glances. How successful had he been?

Again, Tom made a careful answer to what might be a loaded question. It was not for him to say, but Greenock docks were a good place for an evangelist to start. If Christians had a passion for the gospel, God gave them the courage. But if they lacked passion, they'd best give the Clyde a wide berth. The dockers were hard men.

After two hours of questions the members of the board were satisfied that this was a man they could use. But there was a disappointment in store. For political reasons the Sudan was closed and no one could say when it would reopen. The room was silent.

The chairman leaned forward and cleared his throat. 'Dr Cochrane, would you be prepared to consider an alternative posting?'

The answer came quickly. 'On one condition, sir. That you send me to the neediest place there is!' Suddenly there were smiles around the table and the chairman made another proposal. When Tom heard it, he frowned. He had heard of Inner Mongolia, but how on earth did you get there?

\*\*\*

A lot happened in 1896. Early in the year Tom proposed to Grace Greenhill, the dark-haired nurse with whom he had fallen in love. In his diary he wrote a couplet that might have been borrowed from Ibsen's play *A Doll's House*:

> Give me a woman, not a doll,
> a heart that's human, or not at all.

Her heart proved as humanly soft as he could have wished for. In June he took his final examinations and qualified as Dr Cochrane MB CM (Bachelor of Medicine, Master of Surgery). He had completed his training without a single examination failure, a remarkable achievement considering the odds. At the first opportunity, he applied to join the London Missionary Society. In December he and Grace were married.

In this situation, Tom's request to go 'to the neediest place there is' with a young wife seems today like sheer bravado. As a doctor I often wondered what on earth the board members were thinking of when they posted him to Mongolia, the remotest of China's territories and like the other side of the moon. Professionally he was a fledgling; the ink on his parchment was still damp and he had no postgraduate training and no tropical experience. The brief time since qualifying he had spent doing locums to earn a little money. What is more, a newly qualified doctor has a great deal to learn from older physicians, yet the missionary Society posted him to the edge of nowhere without medical or nursing colleagues. Nor had he attended theological college, so he had no training in churchmanship or mission work. He knew nothing of China but was expected to master Mandarin, one of the most difficult languages on earth, while on the job.

The truth, I learned, was that Tom's case was not exceptional. The majority of medical missionaries sent to China in the nineteenth century were single-handed and many were new graduates with only a basic medical education. If similar posts existed today, they would attend Bible college, missionary training school and language school. They would also study for the Diploma in Tropical Medicine and Hygiene and probably have experience in obstetrics, child health and accident medicine.[1]

But Tom Cochrane was a man of extraordinarily strong character. Once he was convinced that God was leading him in a particular direction, nothing would deflect him. One can only conclude that the board members saw that and were prepared to take a gamble on him, and on Grace.

The weeks after they were accepted passed in a frenzy. The Cochranes had to buy everything from medicines to mosquito nets. They took Bibles, tracts, educational material, surgical equipment, dressings, drugs, bedding, clothes and a few small items of furniture. Everything had to be crammed into a trunk and a few small crates. Grace struggled to find room for luxuries like tinned butter, condensed milk and candles.

The Society briefed all its missionaries before they went overseas, but none of the London staff had served in Inner Mongolia, and the couple were left uncomfortably ignorant of what lay on the other side

---

[1] The London Missionary Society did not have a missionary training college until the 1940s, when it established St Andrew's College in Selly Oak (but only for men).

of the world. They had been married barely a month when their families and friends saw them off at Glasgow Central Station. The party included some of Tom's medical chums who probably thought that he had taken leave of his senses.

They sailed from Southampton on 9 January 1897 in a German steamer called the *Preussen*.

\*\*\*

From the junk the Manchurian coast loomed, but it was not the Cochranes' final destination. That was a town called Chaoyang, days away on the other side of the border with Inner Mongolia. Once ashore they exchanged the delights of the junk for those of a pony cart.

Carts had been used for centuries in China. In Mongolia they were drawn by a skinny donkey or a pony with a piece of sacking stretched beneath its tail to catch the precious droppings. Heavier versions were drawn by oxen.

Imagine, then, a dog kennel on wheels with no springs or upholstery, just bare boards, and a roof of woven matting soaked in wood oil to keep off the sun and rain. Imagine travelling long distances in all weathers, sitting cross-legged, jolted around like a sack of flour. Imagine yourself in summer *looking* like a sack of flour as the dust caked your hair and clothes. Tom described travelling in a cart as a 'mild form of martyrdom'.

For a smoother ride, particularly in the hills, a litter suspended between mules was better. Even a wheelbarrow was more comfortable and could travel surprisingly long distances.[2]

There was an old missionary joke: how could a man make himself comfortable when travelling in a pony cart? The answer was that he lined the interior with straw and padded it with as many quilts and furs as he owned. Then he arranged pillows down the sides and

---

[2] The wheelbarrow was both the cart and the carriage of northern China. It had a large wheel set centrally in a sturdy wooden frame and widely spaced handles to which shoulder straps were attached. A strong man could lift half a ton of cargo, or carry two passengers 20 miles in a day. The rates were a quarter of what the railways charged – a good reason for patriotic Chinese to favour the wheelbarrow.

around the back. Then he placed his possessions on top, took his stick and walked beside the pony.

The Cochranes' cart trundled over the coastal plain of vast brown fields where peasants in broad hats sowed crops of soybeans and sorghum to make into flour or syrup. As the foreigners passed by, the villagers straightened up and stared incredulously at them while they stared back. The land was very different from the paintings of southern China back home; there were no emerald-green paddy fields crisscrossed by ridges, no brightly coloured birds darting among bamboo thickets. Grace had expected the waterfalls, willows and ornamental bridges depicted on the Blue Willow plates that were so popular with Glasgow housewives. Here she saw only treeless plains, broken-down villages, and waterwheels turned by pitifully small donkeys.

After crossing the plain they travelled on rutted roads and along dry riverbeds. Grace clutched the side of the cart on the corners. Its jolting mimicked the junk and left her more nauseous than she had been at sea. The villages were ringed by orchards of peaches, apples and pears. On every hilltop the Chinese had built a shrine or a small temple, as if to say 'These are the gods of the hills – bow down before them!' When they looked closer, they found the shrines were dilapidated and peeling. They contained iron dragons that were brown with rust and stone idols with missing limbs. Tom was not impressed.

Grace was intrigued by the appearance of the villagers. The people of the north were taller and sturdier than other Chinese, which (it was said) was because they were wheat eaters, not lowly rice eaters. Their skin was as dark and weathered as their Mongolian neighbours. The men shaved the front of the scalp above the temples and gathered their hair into a pigtail which reached down to the waist. It was a legal requirement under the Manchus and the penalty for not complying was beheading. The only exceptions were condemned criminals who were allowed to grow long hair while awaiting execution. This gave rise to the saying, 'Lose your hair and keep your head, or keep your hair and lose your head.'

The carter was a surly fellow who clamped his pipe between his teeth and muttered to himself as he steered round the gopher holes. Oncoming carters would not give way when they saw he was carrying foreigners. This caused several near misses and a lot of bad language.

At one stop Tom examined their pony with a clinician's eye. Unlike ponies in Scotland, it had a tail which reached almost to the ground. Was this usual, he wondered? He did not speak enough Mandarin to ask, but the carter provided the answer when he plucked some hairs and plaited them together to repair a strap. Later Tom learned that the Mongols made proper ropes from horses' tails which were superior to hemp, particularly in wet weather.

The people were resourceful but did they know how to live properly? The Cochranes' first taste of a Chinese inn did not suggest so. Chinese inns had a reputattion with Europeans that was as odious as that of the Chinese cart. You could get supper and a bed for two coppers, but it was not worth the money. On the first night in Manchuria, Grace was too exhausted to care. 'Tom, just find me a bed,' she moaned.

A dishevelled innkeeper reeking of beer lurched into his courtyard to welcome them. 'All the comforts of my unworthy hostelry are at Your Excellencies' disposal.'

The comforts consisted of a mud-walled room with a mud-beaten floor. The window was covered with squares of translucent paper to which a snooper applied the tip of his tongue and poked a hole in order to spy on them. Around the edge of the room stood large storage jars of vegetables which smelled ancient; in the centre stood the *kang* or bed-stove, a brick platform raised three feet above the floor. The word *kang* means 'to dry' and warmth radiated from the bricks. It came from hot air piped from the stove where food was cooked. The innkeeper fed the stove with grain stalks. As he worked the bellows, acrid smoke leaked from crevices in the *kang* until tears streamed down their faces. 'Are you roasted yet?' he called out cheerfully.

Throughout northern China, families virtually lived on their *kang* during the long winters. It was used for working, eating, entertaining, sleeping, making love, giving birth and dying. The Emperor in his Celestial Palace slept on a *kang* which was reputedly upholstered in silk. Tom discovered that the heat was not evenly distributed and noted, 'There is nothing so uncomfortable that I know of as to lie on a hot *kang* under a torn window on a cold night.' The wind from the steppes, the fumes from the stove, the plunging of animals in the courtyard and the night watchman's drum made sleep anything but easy. During the next three years, Tom often stayed in Chinese inns and on occasion owed his life to their strong walls and gates. But he never came to think warmly of them.

On that first night the innkeeper's wife poured tea from a Russian samovar and served up two bowls of dough strings and a dish of fried bean curds with chopped mutton. It was hardly appetizing, but their hunger overcame their distaste. Later they spread bedding on the *kang* and as they climbed on to it, Grace remarked: 'What a relief, darling! No bedbugs to torment us.' Half an hour later they were scratching furiously. The room was infested with fleas.

An incident two days later showed them how important it was not to cause the Chinese to lose face. Tom tried a few halting words of Mandarin on the cart driver, who scowled and fell to cursing in a curiously staccato way. They worked out that he had a stammer and was furious because he thought they were mimicking him. That night he vanished, vowing to have nothing more to do with foreigners. Fortunately they were able to recruit a more cheerful character, and so they approached Inner Mongolia on the last stage of their journey.

As they went on, the countryside grew browner and bleaker. At that time of year the plains, the hills, the villages and even the trees were the colour of mud. The fields contained shoots which later would grow into crops taller than any seen in Europe. Sorghum (called *gaoliang* in Chinese, meaning 'tall grain') reached a height of ten feet, and bandits would ride through it unseen and attack travellers from the rear. In these remote parts, foreigners were constantly at risk from bandits and from hostile peasants. The further they travelled from the coast, the more ignorant and superstitious the population became.

The wearisome journey took over a week. Later in life Tom marvelled that in the same span of time he could travel by the Trans-Siberian railway and the Eastern Chinese railway from London across Europe, Russia, Siberia and Manchuria to Peking.

At last they saw the battlements of a town in the distance and their driver cracked his whip and shouted a word they understood: 'Chaoyang'. A group of Chinese Christians was waiting to welcome them there.

But first there was another shock. As the cart came closer to the town, Tom spotted poles positioned at regular intervals along the walls. Fixed to each was a severed human head. Some were bleached skulls which grinned a toothy welcome; others were blind and bloody, their eyes picked out by crows. Worst of all, on a pile of refuse and partly eaten by dogs lay the body of a female baby. Tom leaned forward to draw the curtain which separated them from the driver, but he was not quick enough. Grace's face turned white. He put his arm around her as she vomited over the wheel. And so they came to Chaoyang. Its name means 'City Facing the Morning Sun'.

# 2

## *The neediest place on earth*

An American missionary when returning home from China was asked by a newspaper reporter, 'Dr Smith, our readers want the bottom line about the facts in China.' His reply was, 'Sir, there is no bottom and there are no facts.'[1]

What he meant was that China is simply too vast and too diverse for generalizations. The area for which the Cochranes were headed was unlike any other part of the Qing Empire. In the 1890s Inner Mongolia was one of the emptiest and remotest places on the planet, twice the size of France and over a billion square kilometres of windswept plains, mountains and valleys. Its rich mineral deposits had not yet been exploited and it had few towns. Much of the land is semi-desert, but between the mountain ranges there are fluvial planes and basins. Here there are lakes and rivers with marshes rich in plant life and waterfowl. When the moisture levels are high, the grasslands are covered in irises, orchids and roses. The capital city is Hohhot, which means 'Green City' in the Mongolian language.

The Cochranes' destination was in the east, in an area between the great north plain of China and the Gobi Desert. Its borders were fluid and today the city of Chaoyang lies not in Inner Mongolia but within the Chinese province of Liaoning. (In Tom's day it was in the metropolitan province of Zhili or Chihli, now known as Hebei.) To the south lay the Great Wall of China, 'the great Purple Barrier'. Everything north of it was beyond the boundaries of civilization. The imperial troops could not defend this vast territory; there were no

---

[1] He was the Revd Arthur Henderson Smith (1845–1932), a veteran of the American Civil War, who spent 54 years as a missionary in China. He lived through the Siege of the Legations and his book *China in Convulsion* is a detailed contemporary account of that event.

railways and the roads were no more than tracks across the wilderness.

On the plains Mongolian nomads roamed on small fast ponies, protecting their herds of sheep, goats and camels from the weather and the wolves. Much reduced in numbers, they were the proud descendants of Genghis Khan whose cavalry had conquered half the world in the thirteenth century and subjected China to the Mongol yoke.

The sky under which they lived is as vast as the plains, its ever-changing patterns of clouds mirroring the vast flocks of sheep and goats. The yurts, the mushroom-shaped Mongolian tents, look from a distance like miniature cumuli. High overhead, golden eagles wheel and in springtime the sky is filled with larks and migrating cranes.

In the 1890s the land seethed with ethnic hatred. Inner Mongolia was partly a self-governing region within the Chinese Empire, much of it being ruled by princes who wielded absolute power over ancestral lands. They were divided along tribal lines into leagues and banners. Starting in the 1700s, waves of Han Chinese had crossed the Great Wall and seized tracts of arable land illegally. The area north of the wall was called 'the land of the high grass' and it was good soil. Even with poor tools it produced good harvests. The Mongols scorned agriculture and they allowed the Chinese to push them further and further back. This created a complex administrative situation. Chinese prefectures were set up within the Mongol territories and the Han came under their jurisdiction, but the Mongolian princes retained the ownership of the land and its natural resources. There were endless battles over boundaries, and water and timber rights.

As the Manchu dynasty weakened, Chinese tenants refused to pay their taxes to the Mongol rulers. Violence came to a head in 1891 when a Chinese secret society called Jindandao, or 'Way of the Golden Elixir', raised a rebellion which killed 150,000 Mongols and forced another 100,000 to flee north. The Chinese army suppressed the rebellion by meting out savage punishment to both sides.

Chaoyang was on the front line between the factions, and during the Jindandao rebellion the fields around it ran with blood. The town was also constantly exposed to warlords and bandits marauding from the north. Neglected by the Imperial Government and unable to defend itself properly, its people lived in a state of near anarchy. So when

15

Tom asked the Society to send him to the neediest place on earth, he got all that he had bargained for, politically as well as medically.

Around Chaoyang was a plain of 60 square miles where the peasant farmers grew wheat. They laboured hard in the short hot summers and the long cold winters, punished by droughts and sandstorms which blew out of the steppes like whirling dervishes. For seven months in the year the land had little or no rain. The plains ended in a barrier of hills which rose to 2,500 feet. They increased the sense of Chaoyang's isolation from the rest of the world. Tom wrote: 'In my lonely moments I used to gaze at the pagoda-crowned summits as a prisoner might his prison bars.' Travel in the mountains was hazardous; the tracks ran alongside steep chasms and a pony cart could easily get out of control and slide over the edge.

\*\*\*

The mission compound at Chaoyang lay outside the town gates, vulnerable and ill-favoured. Even the Christians thought the spot was bad *feng shui*. Mud walls were no problem to thieves, who greased their bodies with goose fat and stuck needles through their pigtails to prevent them being grabbed and held. A family who possessed anything of value needed a good watchman if they were to sleep soundly.

The mud-built bungalow was small but adequate, and Grace set about making it as attractive as possible. She was a newly wed Scots lass and this was her first home. The local women had cleaned the building to their own standards but it needed a good going-over. She put rattan curtains over the paper windows and rush matting on the bare floor, then went looking for wildflowers. She could do no more until the crates were unpacked.

Of the other buildings, the chapel was not a grand affair: one room with an earthen floor and paper windows. The pews were backless forms. On the first morning, members of the congregation turned up in their best clothes with their children, smiling and bowing to the Cochranes. They pointed proudly to the Bible pictures on the whitewashed walls and to the altar with a simple wooden cross. From a locked box they produced a tattered Chinese Bible as if it were a holy relic.

Next Tom investigated the buildings which he planned to make his dispensary. To a medical missionary, a dispensary was far more than a place where medicines were prepared; it was everything he needed rolled into one – his examination room, treatment room, operating theatre, pharmacy, waiting room and dental surgery.

As he took stock, his heart sank. These were sheds built for pigs. The ceilings were made of grain stalks covered with rice paper, and above them a colony of rats with tails like noodles scampered about. When the rain got in, the paper became sodden and rats, stalks and droppings fell on to anyone standing below. Tom knew that bubonic plague, which is carried by rats, was endemic in Mongolia. There was no question of operating in these conditions. He later wrote:

> It came home to me that I was the only medical man in thousands of
> square miles of bandit-ridden territory and that it would be as much
> as my life was worth if I should happen to perform an unsuccessful
> operation.

He took his troubles to Grace. Why didn't they warn him? He couldn't work in these conditions – they were far too primitive! But she was still shaken by the horrors they had seen on arrival and was not particularly sympathetic. He had asked for the neediest place and he got it. Aye, he shouldn't make a big thing of it, just get on with the job.

\*\*\*

That was the first of many shocks. Back home in Scotland, the name Inner Mongolia had a romantic ring like Coromandel or Timbuktu. But reality was different. When the Cochranes ventured outside the compound, they entered a frighteningly alien world.

Chaoyang was a town of 50,000 inhabitants. It had a long Mongolian history, but now only a tenth of the population were Mongols, with a smattering of Manchurians, Tibetans and Koreans. It had been taken over by the Chinese. The buildings were low mud houses with tiled roofs arranged higgledy-piggledy around a maze of narrow alleys and courtyards. In summer people hung mat awnings across the alleys to ward off the heat.

China's reputation for hygiene in those days stood in marked contrast to her cultural achievements. Every European and American writer seems to have commented on it, some claiming that they could smell the land from 50 miles out to sea. Outside the treaty ports there were no latrines; people emptied their slops into the streets along with rotting vegetables, old rags, animal carcases and even human remains. The mounds of filth formed a perfect breeding ground for dysentery and cholera. In the rainy months they liquefied and flowed everywhere. Pigs and dogs rooted in the muck and naked children played happily, unaware of the dangers.[2]

But there was money in dung, and it was removed, dried and pulverized to fertilize the fields. Human dung, which was particularly rich in ammonia, was more valuable than animal dung, which was dried into cakes and used as *argol* (fuel). It burned warmly and with surprisingly little smoke.

In the summer, dust storms from the steppes enveloped the town, the grit stinging people's eyes, filling their nostrils and making unprotected food uneatable. They scattered fresh sewage to keep down the sand which piled up in the streets. 'It's a matter of choice,' they said. 'You choke on the sand or put up with the smell.'

Chaoyang had changed little from the days of the Mongol Empire. In its teeming streets, people jostled with animals that roamed freely: sheep, goats, pigs, oxen and camels. Everything took place in the open air: people ate and drank, markets were held, hair was cut, shoes were made and saddles mended. Fortune-tellers, chiropodists, pawnbrokers and entertainers competed noisily for custom. The air was full of hammering and the cries of ironmongers, silversmiths and coffin-makers.

Beneath a glass jar of decayed teeth which served as a signboard, a peasant would haggle over the dentist's fee. Everyone stopped to watch the fun. When he yelled in pain, they jeered, 'You should have paid more.'

---

[2] Similar conditions had always existed in European cities which had no waste removal and no thought for hygiene. In the first century AD, the Roman emperor Vespasian was lunching one day when a dog brought in a human hand which it had found in the street, and dropped it under the table. Vespasian took this as a favourable omen, since the hand was considered a symbol of power.

Next to the dentist a Chinese doctor would erect a stall with a banner which promised to cure everything from heartburn to haemorrhoids: 'Dr Lao will relieve all your worries – no pain.' When his back was turned, a young scallywag altered it to read, 'Dr Lao will relieve you of all your savings', and was chased away.

Many of the townspeople had never seen white people before and they found the Cochranes repulsive. They followed them around, making animal noises. In their opinion (which was held by all Chinese) the foreigners' noses were too long, their eyes too round and their skin an ugly red. In addition their speech was barbaric and their manners coarse. What honourable gentleman would be seen in public arm in arm with his wife?

Most of this escaped the Cochranes at the time, as did a small but redeeming point. They were addressed as *iang-ren*, 'foreigners', not *iang kuei-tsi*, 'foreign devils', a term that came with a hiss. But the mockery was tiresome. Tom usually managed a smile in response, but Grace could not hide her feelings. 'We've come to love them and give them hope, haven't we, Tom? Why do they treat us like this?' After a few visits to the town, she found it safer and more pleasant to stay within the compound and to help Tom and John Parker there.

There was one building of substance in Chaoyang, the Longxiang temple, which was home to 300 lamas or Buddhist monks. When Tom went inside, he saw rows of yellow-robed figures sitting cross-legged before a massive golden Buddha. Brocaded streamers hung from the ceiling, and in recesses around the courtyard hundreds of smaller idols were perched on lotus thrones and carved clouds.

The air was blue with the smoke of incense, and the lamas' chanting was broken by the clink of copper as passers-by threw coins into baskets. From time to time bells rang, gongs sounded and shaven heads bent forward. The lamas were the only worshippers and they looked unspeakably bored.

In a courtyard an old woman and a lama screamed obscenities at each other before an altar where the poor left food offerings. She had come to have her fortune told, and now she was expected to donate yak butter for the temple lamps. Whatever glimpse of the future the lama conjured up had failed to please her and she would not part with a penny. As Tom watched the ruckus, the man turned on him, his face twisted in anger. He made a crude gesture that said 'Out!' Tom left quickly. In that moment he realized how ignorant and uncouth the lamas were. It would take time to win them.

\*\*\*

This introduction left Tom wondering how strong the foundations of Christian mission were in Mongolia. In the 1820s the Revd Edward Stallybrass, a member of the London Missionary Society, and two other missionaries had brought the gospel to Siberia and Mongolia and translated the Bible into Mongolian, but they were expelled in 1840 by the tsarist government. Later the London Missionary Society penetrated Mongolia from the south when its missionary James Gilmour arrived in 1871.

Like Tom Cochrane, Gilmour was a sturdy Scot from the Glasgow area and not easily deterred. Anti-Christian riots broke out in Tientsin in June 1870 in which ten nuns and three priests were massacred, the French cathedral destroyed and a war with France narrowly averted. Nonetheless the next month Gilmour set out from Peking with a single guide to cross Mongolia. He developed an amazing itinerant ministry in which he almost became a Mongol. He mastered the language and lived like a nomad, keeping all his possessions in a haversack. He slept in their yurts and ate their millet. He crossed and recrossed the plains, riding ponies the Mongolian way. Later he became fluent in Manchu and Mandarin and adopted Chinese dress.

Some Christians see romance in the life of a missionary like Gilmour and relish it, from a distance, that is. This was tough, dangerous work which brought Gilmour great loneliness. He went for months without seeing another European. In 1874 he was joined by a young wife who came out 'unseen' from England. It proved a love match and for a time she shared his work, but she too paid the price. She died of tuberculosis in 1885, leaving him with three small boys.

Rewards were slow in coming; it took over ten years to win his first convert. During one trip lasting eight months he preached to 24,000 people, yet only two individuals showed an interest.[3] Indeed Gilmour

---

[3] He was not alone in this. *The Chinese Recorder* of 1875 estimated that 409,000 patients had been seen in Canton between 1861 and 1872. Only 12 had been converted.

was criticized for wasting his time on the nomads and in later years he moved to Inner Mongolia to work in the towns and among what he called 'agricultural Mongols'. Chaoyang became his mission centre, with three outstations. When he died of typhus in 1891, he was widely loved and respected.

Gilmour's classic text, *Among the Mongols*, was published in 1883 and its successor, *More about the Mongols*, appeared ten years later; both created much excitement in missionary circles. But Tom had no ambition to copy what he called 'Gilmour's itinerating Mongol labours'. After a few months in China, he wrote:

> I don't think we ought to consume precious time travelling in pursuit of a handful of Mongols who don't wish or won't accept the gospel, when there are thickly populated districts where thousands of souls just as precious as the Mongols are willing to hear and ready to receive the message.

On one matter the men would have agreed: the evangelistic potential of good medical care. The 'mission through medicine' approach was inaugurated in China by Dr Peter Parker (1804–88), its first Protestant medical missionary. It was said that 'he opened China to the gospel at the point of a lancet'. The tradition continued with Benjamin Hobson (1816–73) who worked in Hong Kong and Canton (Guangzhou) and who wrote five basic medical texts in Chinese. Even the renowned James Hudson Taylor (1832–1905) when he had completed his first tour in China made a point of finishing his medical studies.[4]

Gilmour followed this lead. Writing in the *China Medical Missionary Journal* in 1886, he described how he used his medicines 'as a means to an end, to create friendly points of contact with the patient and enable me to convey to them the knowledge of the gospel'. He often travelled to markets and fairs, social events which included horse racing, wrestling and feasting, all of which the Mongols loved. He took a medical kit and applied his common sense to medical and dental problems. In nine months of 1887 he 'treated' between 12,000 and 13,000 patients and saw the suspicions of the people melt away.

---

[4] In the event, Taylor did not practise as a medical missionary, but the China Inland Mission which he founded employed many of them and operated several hospitals.

Later he wrote, 'When I can do so little, what might not a qualified medical man do?' Indeed one wonders what James Gilmour and Tom Cochrane might have achieved together. Gilmour was 47 when he died in 1891; Tom was 31 when he arrived six years later. As a physician Tom had a higher view of medicine, but like Gilmour he did not see it as an end in itself. It was an aid to the gospel, a way to bring people face to face with the love of Jesus. The two would have made a formidable team.

After Gilmour's death, the London Missionary Society sent the Revd John Parker, who was not medically trained, to Chaoyang. He struggled in the chaos that followed the Jindandao rebellion. He had to bury his valuables and flee in December 1892, when many converts were roughly handled and Bibles and tracts were burned. When he returned with a colleague, the Revd William MacFarlane, they resumed the work and conducted the first Christian marriage and the first Christian burial service in the region. MacFarlane suffered repeated attacks of dysentery and returned to England in 1894. That year war broke out with Japan and Chaoyang again became too dangerous, so Parker again fled.

Parker was convinced that there was an open door in Chaoyang for evangelism, but he lacked money and buildings and like MacFarlane he struggled with ill health. He longed for a medical colleague and reported, 'The place here is ripe for a doctor and such an accession would give great impetus to the work.' He bequeathed the Cochranes a congregation of 94 believers and 'enquirers', divided between the town and three outstations. He also leftt a plot of land adjoining the compound. The idea was to build a proper surgery on it, but of course there was no money.

\*\*\*

Most doctors have patients who stand out like milestones – or tombstones – in their memories. In my experience some of these cases redound to the doctor's credit while others do not, but both provide valuable object lessons.

Tom got his first memorable case soon after he arrived in Chaoyang. Grace was preparing supper when a young man burst into the compound. He was a peasant dressed in a thin blue cotton jacket and trousers, cotton socks and cloth shoes with felt soles. His pigtail was coiled under his cap and on seeing Tom he uncoiled it, for it was disrespectful to address a superior without loosening it. Then he dropped to his knees in a kowtow, striking his forehead three times on the floor. He cried out in great distress, '*Taifu, chiu ming. Taifu, chiu ming?*' ('Doctor, save life! Doctor, will you save life?')

The man mimed a woman in labour in what was clearly an urgent plea for help. Tom grabbed his obstetrics bag and within minutes they were off in the man's cart. After an hour of jolting across the plain they came to a village of mud houses and narrow alleys. From one of the houses a wail was going up. A coffin stood on the wooden threshing platform outside.[5]

A young woman lay moribund on a *kang* while the village 'midwife', a crone in a filthy apron, hovered nearby muttering spells and waving incense. Tom pushed her aside and set up a hurricane lamp. The woman had been in obstructed labour for many hours and was past struggling. He administered a few whiffs of what the Chinese called 'dream medicine' and applied his forceps, grateful for the sound obstetric training he had received at the Glasgow Maternity Hospital.

> I immediately took the case in hand, gave the woman chloroform and saved them both. I shall never forget the scene as I left the house. The man and other relatives accompanied me to the door and knelt around me as the sun was setting saying, '*Taifu hsin hao.*' ('The doctor's heart is good.')

Travelling back under a darkening sky, he thought of the countless mothers in villages across Mongolia who had no help when childbirth went wrong and for whom the prospect of spiritual salvation was even more remote. With God's grace, he would save souls as well as lives. A surge of hope filled him whenever he remembered that moment: 'I felt that a nation was waiting to be healed.' He had asked for the neediest place possible and God would not let him down.

Tom Cochrane was young, passionate and resolute. He had committed himself and Grace to ten years on the mission field and in his diary speculated whether all Mongolia might be converted to Christianity in that time.

As yet he had no idea of the darkness that covered the land.

---

[5] When they could afford it, family members had their coffins made and stored in advance. This reduced the chance of a financial crisis if more than one death happened at once.

# 3

## *The Peach Blossom Spring*

To understand what missionaries faced in China in the late nineteenth century, it is necessary to know something of the country's condition. Tom arrived knowing very little. The switch from Africa and the speed of his posting gave him little time to prepare. But he may have been aware of a Chinese fable which dates from the fifth century AD and is called 'The Peach Blossom Spring':

> A young fisherman sailed by chance up a river running through a beautiful forest of peach trees which were in blossom. The source of the river was a spring flowing out of a grotto, through which he squeezed into another world. There he found a village of neat houses surrounded by fertile fields, lakes and orchards. It was a utopia cut off from the outside world. He stayed for a week with the villagers sharing their idyllic existence. When he left they begged him, 'Do not tell outsiders about us!' He did so nonetheless but outsiders never found their way there.

The story is a parable of how China sealed itself off for thousands of years while its people flourished in science, art and agriculture. The nation's best-known achievements were the Four Great Inventions: papermaking, the magnetic compass, gunpowder and printing. But a full list contains hundreds of brilliant and useful discoveries in farming, metallurgy, coal and oil extraction, machine-making, medicine, astronomy, mathematics, porcelain, silk and wine-making.

Thus in agriculture the Chinese were the first people to irrigate and fertilize their fields and to invent the screw pump and the watermill. They domesticated the silkworm and created the finest silks the world has ever known. They were the first to cultivate rice, tea, peaches, apricots, and many flowering shrubs and medicinal plants. In architecture they invented the arch bridge and built the Great Wall which stretches in all its forms for over 10,000 miles; they also dug the shorter and less-known but more useful Grand Canal. In the realm of art they created exquisite works in bronze and brought porcelain to the pinnacle of perfection. Their artists painted amazing likenesses of birds, animals and flowers and invented three-dimensional landscapes. In literature they gave the world encyclopaedias, dictionaries, history books, poetry and essays. They invented tuned bells, reed organs, chamber music and opera. They produced things as diverse as paper money, alcoholic beverages, bellows, blast furnaces, kites, matches, umbrellas and spectacles.

The achievements which concerned Tom Cochrane most were in medicine and pharmacy. This too was part of the Peach Blossom Spring, a time when physicians were scholarly and saintly. Chinese medicine had been systematized as far back as the Chou dynasty (approximately 1120–250 BC). A compendium of *materia medica* written in 1578 remains the most comprehensive record of traditional medicine ever produced. Its 52 volumes contain nearly 2,000 entries of all the plants, animals, minerals and other items which were believed to have medicinal properties. It is still in print and used as a reference today.

But medicine had stagnated over the centuries; the writings that Chinese doctors consulted were centuries old. There were no scientific observations, no experiments and no anatomical dissections, so knowledge did not progress. A Chinese doctor in 1900 knew less anatomy, physiology and medicine than a Greek physician in the time of Hippocrates. He knew a great deal about the medicinal properties of plants, but little about the diseases for which they were used.

The list of China's achievements must be weighed against the other side of the story – the nation's monumental conceit. China became the cynosure of all eyes, the source of all goodness and wisdom. It gave itself the name 'the Middle Kingdom', that is, a place at the centre of the universe between heaven and earth. All the nations of the East, from the Himalayas to the jungles of Vietnam, came to bow down and pay homage to the Emperor, the Son of Heaven. The Chinese word for an ambassador meant a tribute bearer.

When Western merchants started to arrive off China's coasts, the Manchu emperors believed that they could conduct as much or as little business with them as they wished. They described them in documents as *yi*, the Chinese character for barbarians, and imposed firm trade restrictions. But the barbarians had come halfway round the world and once they tasted the riches of the Orient there was no stopping them. The genie would not squeeze back into the bottle.

In a famous debacle, the British government sent a trade embassy to Peking in 1793 under Lord George Macartney to negotiate trade concessions with the Qianlong Emperor. The precise details are unclear, but during his audiences Macartney refused to perform a grand kowtow. This practice (known in Chinese pidgin as 'knockee head') meant prostrating oneself and knocking one's forehead on the ground a total of nine times.

This proved far too much for His Lordship and indeed all later British envoys. He returned home empty-handed and the Emperor wrote caustically to King George III: 'Our Celestial Empire possesses all things in prolific abundance and lacks no product within its borders. There is therefore no need to import the manufactures of outside barbarians in exchange for our own produce.' An important opportunity to develop Anglo-Chinese trade in an equitable manner was missed. Soon adventurers and opium smugglers caused the *cordon sanitaire* created around the Qing Empire to crumble, though as late as 1840 the only place where a foreigner could legally set foot (apart from the Portuguese port of Macau) was a waterfront in Canton known as the Thirteen Factories.

The trading tensions came to a head with the Opium War of 1839–42, which lobbyists in Westminster portrayed as a 'just war' in defence of free trade. After it ended, China was gradually prised open like a rusty gate. Britain's appropriation of Hong Kong as a trading base in January 1841 was only the beginning. China was forced to accept further treaty ports at Shanghai, Canton, Amoy and Fuchow. After the Second Opium War (1856–60) seven more ports were extorted, including three inland locations on the Yangtze River. By 1906 there were a total of 38 treaty ports and they accommodated 1,837 foreign firms, 40,000 foreign residents and seven million Chinese who lived under foreign protection.

These settlements were mini-colonies where foreigners operated under their own laws and municipal government. They had a customs house, a business sector, a police force, a judiciary, and often a garrison or naval presence. They cleared out the opium dens, gambling houses and brothels to build European-style dwellings, offices and warehouses and the trappings of empire: clubs, hotels, churches, parks, libraries, schools, mission stations, newspapers and racecourses. The treaty ports had modern water supplies and sewage disposal at a time when China had neither; soon the roads would be metalled and the streets lit with electricity.

From a Western perspective the settlements represented progress and prosperity, but to the Chinese they were a huge affront to national pride and sovereignty, and a disastrous loss of face. But the government was powerless to resist them. Halfway between the two opium wars the Great Taiping Rebellion broke out. Few people today have heard of it. It was the second bloodiest conflict in history and caused the deaths of 20 million Chinese. The struggle raged between 1850 and 1864 and left the Manchus too weak to defend China's sacred soil without European intervention.

A turning point for the Great Powers came in 1860. After an Anglo-French punitive expedition had burned down the Summer Palace outside Peking, the Imperial Government was forced to permit the establishment of embassies in the capital and of consulates in the treaty ports. (Previously this had been denied because such facilities implied equality between nations. By 1867 Britain had 13.) Then, after pressure from the French, the long-standing restrictions on travel into the interior were lifted. This did not trigger the equivalent of a gold rush by Europeans as is sometimes claimed, but their *compradores* (Chinese partner companies and agents) lost no time in exploring the interior, largely for their own profit. The treaty ports became bridgeheads from which China's mineral wealth, particularly the extent of its coal and iron ore deposits, was discovered. Mining companies started up and were followed by concessions for railway companies, river steamers, telegraph lines, steel foundries and factories.

The one group of Europeans that ventured into the interior in ever increasing numbers were the missionaries. In 1865 when James

Hudson Taylor founded a society to evangelize the unreached interior, he named it the China Inland Mission Society.

The response of the Chinese people to these intrusions depended on where they lived. Ninety-seven per cent of the population lived in villages across China's vast plains, hills and valleys. They were conservative, illiterate and intolerant. As late as 1900 most of them had never seen a Westerner. From their viewpoint, their land was being 'plundered' by the foreign barbarians. The degree of economic harm actually done is debatable, but the argument has proved politically useful to Communist leaders down to the present day.

The 'fire carts' are a good example. The Chinese peasants can hardly be blamed for fearing the railways; even in Britain their arrival had caused concern. People thought that the noise and appearance of Stephenson's *Rocket*, which travelled at 35 miles per hour, would create great stress in farm animals as it passed by, causing cows to dry up and hens to cease laying eggs. Most of the nation's horses would end up in the knackers' yards.

Chinese peasants entertained these and greater fears; the engineers could not lay a mile of track without (it seemed) desecrating an ancestral graveyard and disturbing the spirits. And while railways might bring prosperity to a few and increase employment in the long term, they threatened the immediate livelihood of many: carters, muleteers, chair-bearers, wheelbarrow coolies and innkeepers. The railway companies doubtless had sinister motives too: they could move foreign troops and munitions around the country swiftly and smoothly.

Small wonder then that missionaries on remote country stations encountered a wall of hostility and suspicion that often exploded into violence. But in the treaty ports the story was different. The Chinese genius for business meant that foreigners had never lacked for 'hongs' (rented factories and business premises) and *compradores*. As trade and commerce flourished, they needed more partners. They needed Chinese labour, Chinese interpreters and Chinese know-how for the collection of raw materials and the distribution of goods. Above all they needed Chinese capital and they looked increasingly to investors in Shanghai and Canton rather than to London or Paris.

Nor were all Chinese opposed to Western science and technology; as great inventors themselves, they were fascinated by it. Many saw the advantages for agriculture, transport and communications. There were fortunes to be made and great benefits for the nation. When a Northern Irishman, Robert Hart, was appointed Inspector-General of the Imperial Maritime Customs Service in 1863, there was an astronomical leap in government revenue. He held the post until 1910 and ploughed much of the revenue back into maritime surveys and charts. He commissioned a network of lighthouses which made China's treacherous coastal waters far safer. In 1878 he also set up the Chinese Post Office. Meanwhile China ended her centuries-old seclusion by sending missions and individual students abroad to study Western society. A Western-style press and a new student intelligentsia began to emerge.

In a word, many educated Chinese embraced the changes and profited from them. And like it or not, their rulers needed the West, but for different reasons. They needed their weapons, and not just a few Lee Enfield rifles and Armstrong guns, but whole arsenals and navy yards crammed with modern ordnance.

***

Unfortunately, the attitude of most British in China constantly marred the relationship between the two nations. The merchants, the military and even (alas, on occasion) the missionaries were colonialist and imperialist. The British position was straightforward: they possessed the greatest empire in modern history and always dealt robustly with 'the natives' in other lands, albeit having the natives' interests in mind. Why (they argued) should they act differently in China? Britannia's dignity and honour were paramount and demanded the highest respect.

This infuriated and confused the Manchu rulers. They were accustomed to regarding themselves as superior to all other races: the Han Chinese, other Asiatic peoples and above all the foreign barbarians! It was a situation charged with mutual contempt and arrogance.

The British policy was to turn the privileges which had been extracted at gunpoint through what later Chinese historians have called the 'unequal treaties' into inalienable rights. Any infringement of treaty rights, any loss of British life or property, and any slight to the

Union Jack would be punished. Apologies and financial reparations would be demanded, offenders arrested and existing rights reaffirmed. Then, needless to say, a set of new demands would be made.

By a mixture of bullying, threats and reprisals Britain became China's greatest tormentor. 'Torment' is not too strong a word. For soon the Europeans were not satisfied with ports and concessions; military campaigns resulted in the loss of large tracts of land which had belonged either to China or to vassal countries under its protection. China lost territory to Russia in Turkestan, Manchuria and elsewhere on its north-eastern border; it lost its hegemony in Burma to the British and in Vietnam to France (which renamed it French Indo-China); it lost Korea and Taiwan to the Japanese. It was saddled with new borders of 5,000 miles, 2,000 miles and 700 miles controlled by Russia, Britain and France respectively. One Chinese statesman lamented, 'It is an unprecedented situation in the history of more than three thousand years.' It slipped his memory that the Middle Kingdom had been conquered by both Mongols and Manchus long before.

As the end of the century approached, the Europeans scrambled for 'spheres of influence' in China. Germany demanded exclusive trading rights in Shantung (Shandong) province, Russia in Manchuria, Japan in Fukien (Fujian) and Britain in the Yangtze Valley. Thirteen of China's 18 provinces and three in Manchuria were carved up in this way.

The hardest blow fell in 1894, three years before the Cochranes arrived in Inner Mongolia, when China fought a disastrous war with Japan. The Chinese armies marched out through the Victory Gate in Peking to the thunder of an imperial edict: 'The dwarves have rebelled, but there are few of them. Let them be surrounded!' The survivors returned to tell how the Japanese had become invincible by adopting Western weapons and organization. The blood-curdling cries of the Emperor's tiger troops, with their yellow-and-black striped uniforms and painted faces, had failed to frighten the foe.

For the first time in its history, China had been defeated by another Asiatic power, and by a vassal nation with only a tenth of its population. China was beaten on land and at sea. It lost control of Korea, and its greatest offshore possession, Taiwan (Formosa, which means 'beautiful' in Spanish), was lost to the Japanese until 1945.

The war of 1894 finished China as a regional power. It was now the sick man of Asia and its break-up seemed imminent. This encouraged Britain, Russia, France and Germany to extract further concessions on the flimsiest of pretexts. By 1900 virtually every strategic bay and headland was in foreign hands. China's humiliation was complete. Cartoonists depicted the Great Powers crowding around a table and carving up a pie, though it is doubtful whether they seriously considered China's partition, except perhaps in St Petersburg or Tokyo.

*The Great Powers carving up the pie of China; a French cartoon of the 1890s*

\*\*\*

Britain was the greatest thorn in China's side not purely because of its colonialist stance. It handled 60 per cent of China's foreign trade and it dominated the trade in opium. Britain was the biggest, the most efficient and the most ruthless supplier of the drug.[1]

Historically the Chinese had only a modest use for opium, primarily as an analgesic and sedative. But the sheer volume of high-quality opium coming from British India ensnared millions. Some estimates say that by the end of the nineteenth century, a quarter of the population was addicted; in Shanxi province the figure was nearly 90 per cent. The effects were described in the 1890s by a celebrated governor-general, Chang Chih-tung, in a treatise titled *China's Only Hope*. After quoting Confucius, 'Know what your shame is and you will not be far from heroism', he lamented that in reality the Chinese appeared to have no shame in the matter:

> The poison enfeebles the will, saps the strength of the body, renders the consumer incapable of performing his regular duties and unfit for travel from one place to another ... Unless something is done soon to arrest this awful scourge in its devastating march, the Chinese people will be transformed into satyrs and devils. This is the present condition of the country.

Educated Chinese drew comparisons between their country and Japan, which had embraced modern Western ways so efficiently that by the 1890s it was the leading power in the Far East. China, they said, would never regain its supremacy so long as it was in the grip of opium.

Tom Cochrane had many patients in Chaoyang and Peking whose lives were ruined by opium, and he found Britain's involvement in the trade a source of deep shame. People who have lived through the explosion of the drug culture in the West and seen its effects will know how he felt. It made him more resolved than ever to show the love of Christ to the Chinese people.

Today Britain's opium history is no more than a footnote in the West but it is far from forgotten in China, where it is perpetuated in school books and Communist literature. Visitors to China do well to remember that.

\*\*\*

---

[1] See Appendix 2 for more on the opium trade and its consequences.

Tom Cochrane soon learned another unfortunate reality for missionaries. Anti-Western feeling was also anti-religious because all Westerners were viewed as Christian, including atheists, agnostics, humanists, drunkards and the traders who forced the 'foreign smoke' on the people. In 1826 the Daoguang Emperor, whose resistance precipitated the First Opium War, revived an old law regarding 'Wizards, Witches and All Superstitions'. It condemned any foreigner who spread Christianity to death by strangulation, and their converts to a life of slavery in the Muslim territories of the north-west.

The Peking convention of 1860, which opened up the interior, also forced the emperor to reverse that policy. Freedom of religion was conceded but the Christian gospel remained anathema. How (the Chinese argued) could a message of love proceed from such people? How could an unclean thing bring forth a clean thing? The merchants poisoned their victims with opium and the missionaries lectured them on virtue. What hypocrisy! In Britain opium was regarded as poison and the country had laws to control it. A Chinese nobleman once wrote, 'Take away your missionaries and your opium and you will be welcome.' But the truth was there were plenty of reasons apart from opium for hating Christians. The first was their teaching. It is hard to discredit a doctrine of love and forgiveness, and the Chinese desperately needed what the missionaries had to offer, but to Chinese minds the virgin birth was a scandal and the idea of a father sacrificing his son an obscenity. The priests argued that Christian teaching offended China's gods and brought wrath on the land.

Missionaries were accused of practising magic and divination, of causing droughts and of depraved rituals. As early as 1861 a notorious tract, *Bixie Zhishi* ('A Record of Facts to Ward Off Heterodoxy'), alleged all manner of scatological and sexual perversions among Christians. It was reprinted and recirculated many times. In the 1890s pamphlets and pictures ridiculed 'the pig religion'. A booklet titled *Death to the Devil Religion* was distributed free in Hunan province. A missionary commented, 'It is impossible to convey in print any adequate conception of the vile nature of this production.' It contained pornographic drawings of a pig being crucified on the orders of a mandarin, while goat-headed foreigners were simultaneously decapitated.

Notwithstanding the delicacy of their situation, some missionaries showed an extraordinary lack of tact when dealing with 'the natives'. They meddled in local customs and used their position to preach against practices like infanticide, foot-binding and the keeping of concubines, and against the criminal code. This did not make them popular.[2]

The secular pretensions of the Roman Catholic Church were a case in point. The origin of Catholicism in China went back to the sixteenth century when Jesuits from Portugal, Italy, Belgium, Germany and Spain introduced astronomy, calendars, mathematics, hydraulics, geography and map-making. King Louis XIV sent a separate French Jesuit mission in 1685. As the Catholic faith spread, it became increasingly political. Bishops assumed the trappings of rank that belonged to governors: the mandarin's button, the chair-bearers, the outriders and the umbrella of honour. Cannons were fired to salute their arrival and departure.

Catholic priests repeatedly interfered in land disputes on behalf of their congregations and even sat alongside the magistrates. If they lost a case, they appealed to their consulates on the grounds of persecution and the judgement was reversed. They bought up land for cathedrals and churches, whose spires were said by local people to invade the spirit realm and cause bad *feng shui*. One Chinese diplomat likened the situation to erecting a hideous tannery alongside Westminster Abbey. The British legation in Peking warned that, 'Chinese prejudice and superstitions should be more carefully considered in the forms and heights of the buildings erected.'

Missionaries also created financial grievances. Converts were forbidden to take part in idolatrous practices, which meant they were exempt from the taxes used to maintain temples and priests. They paid nothing towards the ceremonies and theatrical performances which were a large part of village life. Since the taxes were assessed village by village, an unequal burden fell on any community where the gospel

---

[2] An early meddler was the Revd Issachar Roberts, an American Baptist minister who played a part in the disastrous Taiping Rebellion. For a short time he was teacher and adviser to Hong Xiuquan, the messianic leader of the 'Heavenly Kingdom' movement which caused the deaths of millions of peasants.

was growing. The converts, who became known as 'rice Christians', were challenged to recant or take the consequences.[3]

In September 1886 a former British minister to China, Sir Rutherford Alcock, wrote a letter to the London *Times* headed 'France, China and the Vatican', in which he vehemently denounced the interference by Catholic priests in China's affairs. They were responsible, he said, for 'the perennial hostility towards Christianity and its teachers in every form, which now pervades the whole nation, rulers and people, from the highest to the lowest'.

The Catholics might bear the brunt, but the Protestants shared the odium. The treaty of 1860 which gave freedom of movement and of evangelism was designed for Catholics, but Protestant missionaries naturally also benefited as protégés of the colonialist system. In any event most Chinese did not distinguish between sects or nationalities.

The opium trade, the interference in local customs, the insults to the gods, the unfair privileges, the Catholics' pretensions, the Protestants' insensitivities . . . the list was a long one. Many grievances were fancied rather than real but they all created unrest. In the last decade of the century, anti-Christian riots and murders occurred in every one of China's 18 main provinces.

\*\*\*

As has been emphasized, in the East it is of great importance not to lose face. Despite every humiliation inflicted on them, the common people (the *laobaixing* or 'old hundred families' as Chinese writers called them) never ceased to believe in their superiority. Nor did they abandon their dreams of a glorious restoration. One day (they told themselves) the slumbering dragon would awake, the barbarians would be driven into the sea, and the Peach Blossom Spring would flower again. In this way they held on to their pride and kept their face intact. It was all moonshine, of course, but it was the stuff of which popular uprisings are made, as the Cochranes would discover to their cost.

---

[3] Brewer's *Dictionary of Phrase and Fable* first recorded the term in 1898 to describe those who professed to be Christian for material benefits, such as a supply of free rice.

# 4

## *The medical ropes*

When Tom asked the London Missionary Society to send him to the neediest place on earth, he got all that he asked for. Once the news of his arrival spread, those who remembered John Gilmour and were physically capable made their way to the mission compound. They came on crutches, on litters, clinging to backs and doubled up in wheelbarrows. Some came very long distances. Tom wrote:

> A favourite way of conveying a patient was upon one leaf of a two-leafed door which is so common in Chinese houses. The sick man or woman was laid upon this and covered with a quilt. Ropes were passed under the door and then over poles supported on two or four men's shoulders and the journey of perhaps a hundred miles was begun.

That was just the start of a sick person's problems. With the expense of the inns, the carriers and food for the journey, the savings of a lifetime could be spent by the time the invalid reached the destination. He or she was now penniless in a strange town and in need of free bed and board. But even if Tom could provide them, the patient only counted on staying two days at most. At home there were fields to be tended and a harvest to gather. If the bearers did not return home quickly, people would starve that winter. No wonder that Tom wrote:

> I used to dread the sight of these bearers lest I should find the patient utterly beyond hope as I frequently did, and in those days it was so risky to have people die in hospital. It was heartbreaking to say 'too late' when one knew the sacrifices which the long journeys had involved.

Among those 'too late' patients was a man who carried his wife on his back across country for 80 miles, only for Tom to tell him she was dying. Another was a young woman carrying a child in her arms who was blue and gasping, dying of diphtheria. The death rate was daunting for a young doctor a year out of medical school, and Tom felt very alone. He recalled wryly that before leaving England he had walked the length of Harley Street and counted the brass plates of over 200 surgeons and physicians. In Chaoyang there was no colleague to whom he could turn for advice:

> To the West of me there were no doctors nearer than Europe; to the North none save in Siberia. To the East one might have been found after two or three days' travelling. After five days' travelling, one would probably have been found in the South.

How did he cope? How did he not panic? As novices, doctors learn quickly from their mistakes, but Tom had to proceed cautiously and not risk too many. There were no police in Chaoyang and if a patient died, his life would be in danger. For months he performed only minor operations.[1]

Tom was conscious that there were no effective cures for most infections. The age of antisepsis had dawned, but in the 1890s there was only symptomatic treatment for typhoid, typhus, tetanus, plague, cholera, tuberculosis, rabies, smallpox, leprosy and diphtheria. Nonetheless exaggerated stories of his success drew patients in great numbers, especially when they heard that he charged nothing.

He soon came into contact with traditional Chinese doctors. The common people had a mixed relationship with these practitioners, who looked wise and scholarly in their long gowns and silk caps. But when things went wrong, as they frequently did, they were scathing about their uselessness and greed. Many were rejects of the Civil Service examinations. Any quack could set himself up without training, and a prudent patient never resorted to a doctor whose family had not been in the profession for three generations. The role was often handed down from father to son.

The reputations of the traditional doctors depended on herbal remedies whose ingredients were a closely guarded secret. Western doctors

---

[1] A decade later Dr Edward Hume, a Yale graduate, found himself in the same situation in Changsha in Hunan province. A patient died shortly after an operation and the situation was so tense that soldiers were sent to protect the foreigners. Things calmed down after Hume bought a very expensive coffin and offered to foot the funeral bill.

who analysed the potions were not impressed. In 1906 the *Chinese Medical Missionary Journal* reported, 'Anything that is thoroughly disgusting in the three kingdoms [i.e. animal, vegetable and mineral] is considered good for medicinal use.' It turned out that the ingredients included cockroaches, moths, toads, lizards, centipedes, caterpillars, cicadas, oyster shells, asbestos, fossils, calomel, rhubarb, animal bile and human excrement. In addition the potions contained powerful plant products, some of which were beneficial. One prescription that Tom found contained 150 different ingredients. That, he concluded, was to ensure that at least one hit the mark.

The Chinese doctors knew a great deal about their plants, but little about strengths and proportions and they left dosages to a patient's discretion. This was dangerous because patients believed that the fouler a medicine tasted and the quicker you drank it, the quicker you got better. They took double doses of liquid medicines – and Chinese doses were large – and when given pills they downed them all at once. Tom learned to dispense in small quantities, which did not please his patients who thought he was being mean. Some medicines were too dangerous to give without supervision.

His patients knew nothing about how their bodies worked. Ancestor worship made it a criminal offence to dissect a corpse, so Chinese doctors were ignorant of anatomy and internal medicine. There was a well-known story of a man who was shot by an arrow which stuck in his side. He went to a doctor who claimed to have surgical expertise and who used a saw to remove the protruding part. 'What you need now', he said, 'is an expert in internal medicine.' The joke was that there was no such person.

Science had little part in diagnosis; it was based on the pulse, which the Chinese claimed to take at no fewer than 98 sites, and on an examination of the tongue. Treatment other than by potions and charms was mainly by acupuncture, which aimed to restore the balance between the *yin* and the *yang*. Some practitioners recommended the use of opium, which did little for their patients' health.

Tom also learned that most illnesses, particularly disfiguring ones like leprosy and smallpox, were attributed to evil spirits. For that reason the Chinese doctors spent as much time studying the magic arts as they did medicine. Sick people were often objects of fear rather than of compassion; in an epidemic they were abandoned to their fate. Thus when Tom cured a patient, he was hailed as 'defeating the devil' and the people were readier to believe in a God who was kind and good. But it was a slow process.

Mental illness was in a category on its own. Several times Tom was asked to visit a house and found a patient who was clinically insane, chained in a darkened room. If left to wander the streets, he was mocked and stoned. If he did anything wrong he was thrown into prison. There was one asylum for the mentally ill in the whole of China. It was opened in 1898 by Dr John Kerr, an American missionary in Canton, 1,200 miles from Chaoyang.

\*\*\*

We have already noted that the people had little instinct for cleanliness, and why should they? No one had taught them that cholera lurked in the dung piles, that fleas carried plague or that lice carried typhus. They listened politely when Tom tried to teach them but they were unconvinced. These were foreign notions – who could say if they were true? Every household had at least one dog and dogs caught water madness, but everyone knew it was evil spirits, not the dogs, that caused children to die.

Even when they tried to protect themselves, the Chinese did so half-heartedly because they did not understand the underlying principles. For example, they had practised smallpox inoculation for generations before Edward Jenner read his paper to the Royal Society in 1797, but superstition forbade them to do it in winter when most cases occurred. Tom frequently saw children with discharging pustules, but their parents made no effort to cover them over, despite his pleas.

Yet there was a positive side to the Chinese life, which was healthier than that of most foreigners. They ate simpler foods (which were usually well cooked), kept better hours, worried less, drank weak tea infusions made with boiling water and generally tried to take care of themselves. Rice was the mainstay in south China, and millet and wheat in the north. A diet which was rich in vegetables and cereals and low in animal protein produced few complications other than flatulence. The Han Chinese in Chaoyang were contemptuous of the Mongolians, whose diet was rich in fat, milk and mutton.

Both races suffered greatly from China's three great killers: tuberculosis (which was universal), syphilis and hookworm. Smallpox and leprosy were also endemic. Other common problems included diphtheria, rabies, arthritis, rheumatism, respiratory infections, anaemias, thyroid disorders, eye diseases and parasites. When epidemics struck, people went down like flies. To these must be added misadventures like burns, fractures, stabbings and gunshot wounds. The ultimate yardstick of health is life expectation and when Tom arrived in Inner Mongolia, few villagers reached the age of 30. He estimated the infant mortality rate at around 600 to 700 per 1,000 live births. (There were no government statistics.) In Britain at the time it was 160.

James Gilmour had summarized the situation laconically: 'The facts that the nation lives out of doors, that it does not drink milk at all and that it never drinks cold water, are responsible for it being "still around".'

The people in Chaoyang were philosophical and claimed they were far better off than the barbarians. 'They feast three times a day till they bulge like buffaloes. Then they die of gluttony and their friends say the climate killed them.'

\*\*\*

Tom's priority was to learn enough Chinese to provide basic medical treatment. Most of the locals spoke Mandarin and he had taken a few lessons in Glasgow, but he had only a few words, his pronunciation was hopeless and he was soon struggling. His patients were not surprised. They had always known that barbarians were incapable of learning their sublime language. Not long ago it had been a criminal offence to teach them. Why should they bother now?

In the dispensary Tom discovered that the Chinese did not use right and left. They described everything by that cherished invention, the magnetic compass. A man might complain of a sharp pain near his navel and when he was palpated for appendicitis he would cry out, 'No, no, south-west of that!' Tom learned to carry a compass in his head.

Fortunately help appeared at the dispensary door. It was Lien-yi, a local evangelist trained by John Gilmour and the best he had. He was particularly valuable as an interpreter because he spoke Mongolian as well as Mandarin. Something about Tom and Grace touched the man's heart and he offered to serve them in any way they wanted. Lien-yi was like manna from heaven and Tom habitually referred to him as 'Mister Heaven'.

He was a cheery character with a dirty round cap jammed over his coiled pigtail, who grinned constantly as if life was one delightful joke. Tom described him as

> one of the most loyal and faithful souls who ever breathed. His sense of humour was invaluable. Many a hearty laugh he gave me, and the man who can make one laugh in days of strain is a friend indeed.

Lien-yi became very attached to the Cochrane household, teaching Mandarin, interpreting in the dispensary and taking on most of the evangelism. It was a strange partnership between a Scottish graduate and a Chinese hedge-preacher. The man had a compassion for his own people which surprised Tom, who had been told that it was not a strong Chinese trait. In the months that followed, Grace would find Lien-yi and Tom together whenever they had a spare moment, Lien-yi gesticulating to parts of his anatomy with one hand while painting Chinese ideograms in the air with the other. It was hard going because many words in Mandarin sound identical and are distinguished only by intonation and context. It takes four times as long to learn Mandarin as a European language.

Fortunately Tom had a natural gift for languages and soon he was able to answer simple questions like, '*Taifu*, what am I suffering from? What can you do about it? When will I be better?' Grace never learned more than a few phrases of Chinese, but she spoke with quiet confidence to the women who came to the dispensary. On their part they quickly accepted this gentle individual who was uncomplaining in the summer heat. By now she was heavy with child. (Her nausea on the journey to Chaoyang had turned out to be more than travel sickness.) They fingered her clothing and asked intimate questions, at which she smiled but often gave no answer.

The women relaxed in the atmosphere of love and acceptance which the Cochranes created, and murmured: 'We never find this feeling anywhere else, not even in our mothers' homes.'

Meanwhile there was a baby coming and Grace found a houseboy to take charge of the kitchen. She had decided not to employ an *amah*. Chinese hygiene had a long way to go before she would entrust her baby to one. The matter of a medical assistant was more pressing, since Grace could no longer help Tom in the dispensary. Mister Heaven found a farmer's son fresh from the fields. He dropped straw on the dispensary floor and fiddled with his cap when Tom questioned him.

At first Tom was not sure about Liu-i. His main ambition in life seemed to be to grow his nails long, ostensibly to scoop up powder and stir potions. Long nails were a mark of superiority; they showed that a man did not earn his living by manual labour. Tom insisted on short nails in the dispensary and once that was settled, he began to teach his new apprentice the rules of basic hygiene.

The question of premises was not solved so easily. The outhouses needed extensive work before they were fit for use. Tom wrote urgently to his Home Board about the situation. It seemed not to have occurred to the members that a doctor would need better facilities than a non-medical man; at this time the London Missionary Society maintained over 60 missionaries in China and only nine of them were medical.

Communications with England were perilously slow. There was no telegraph and it took up to four months to send a letter to London and get an answer. Often Tom felt like a battalion commander cut off from headquarters. He needed to take decisions within hours, not months. When law and order deteriorated, he looked less to his employers for answers and more to his Chinese friends. In the event, it was that which saved him and his family.

In spite of his preoccupation with learning Mandarin, in the first six months Tom saw over 5,600 patients in the dispensary and many others who were too sick to attend. The visits to their homes were an agreeable surprise. In his first annual report he wrote, 'I expected distrust and unwillingness to allow a foreigner entrance to the house; I have been welcomed and invited to rest and drink and been otherwise politely treated.' It was encouraging, too, while dressing a weeping sore to hear again, 'The doctor's heart is good.'

\*\*\*

That autumn Tom somehow refurbished part of the dispensary and started to admit patients for surgery. He had no specialist experience, but his undergraduate training in Glasgow had been thorough.[2] Most of the operations he performed in the dispensary were on the head, neck and limbs. Even in Europe it was still considered too dangerous to open the body cavities. In 1882 Leon Gambetta, the French prime minister, endured four weeks of appendicitis while France's finest doctors stood around arguing. He died without an operation. Twenty years later King Edward VII nearly suffered the same fate through his own stubbornness.

By and large the Chinese were enthusiastic about surgery, especially when it brought quick results which they called 'cut knife miracles'. But the demand meant that a doctor had less time for internal medicine which required longer examinations and unhurried decisions. Tom was often forced to make a quick physical appraisal and take a stab at the diagnosis, hoping that he was right.

He was always pleased to operate on conditions which people thought were caused by witchcraft. Resetting fractures, releasing scar contractures and removing cataracts (which were common in Inner Mongolia) were examples. Cataract extraction is one of the most beautiful operations in surgery and its results are dramatic. One man had gone totally blind before he set out with a guide on the journey to Chaoyang. He had heard that foreign doctors performed amazing cures, but he also heard a rumour that they removed healthy eyes and pounded them into a paste with which they coated the inside of black boxes. With these they created amazing pictures of people and places.

---

[2] Sir Joseph Lister, 'the father of antisepsis', was professor of surgery in the 1860s and put the medical school at the forefront of the specialty. Glasgow also boasted the first X-ray department in the country, not that that was of any value to Tom in Inner Mongolia.

At the last moment the man panicked and tried to run out of the dispensary, but his friend grabbed him and held him back. 'Don't be a fool. You're blind anyway; he can't do you any harm.'

The day after the procedure, Tom darkened the room before removing the bandages. He held his hand in front of the patient's face and asked him to count his fingers. When the man realized that his vision was restored, the look on his face was one of Tom's sweetest experiences. 'I can see! I can see! I can see!' was all he could say.

Another young man walked 25 miles, terrified that he too was going blind. Tom described the scene:

> He took the lotion and the ointment which I gave him and, placing the ointment on one side and the lotion on the other, he reverently knelt between them. In a way most touching to behold, he poured out his heart in gratitude to the God of whom he had been hearing for the prospect of relief of pain and threatened blindness.

After cures like these, everyone who heard about them – householders, traders, peasants, nomads and priests – began asking questions. 'What idol can do anything like this? Which of our gods ever delivered us from trouble?' They hung around the compound, hoping to see a miracle. The chapel filled up for morning and evening services. Tom's skills and compassion began to have effects. He had little time for preaching, but the medicines he dispensed were wrapped in paper printed with Gospel verses.

When the waiting room was full, the patients spilled out into the compound. They rarely came alone; they brought their children, their aunts and uncles, their cousins and their friends. The hours of waiting were a social event. They chatted, cooked meals and played *mah jong* and chess, eating coloured sugar jellies and chewing sunflower seeds. For Mister Heaven this was a grand opportunity for what missionaries called 'wayside sowing'. He moved among the crowd, giving out tracts and Gospels to the literate. To the children he gave picture cards of biblical persons with short descriptions of their lives. He spent hours answering questions that were religious, social and educational. The Chinese are good listeners and even those who came only for free medicine heard him respectfully.

When Tom started work, people jostled forward, thrusting their sores and ulcers in his face. The smell of unwashed bodies was overpowering, but he learned to disguise his feelings and not to hold back. The people watched silently as he gently bathed wounds which their own doctors would not touch. Once, after watching him for a while, a woman whispered, 'Isn't his hand light? Isn't his touch soft?' Another replied, 'This is what we'd expect if Buddha came to earth.'

In his later life Tom used to quote a poem, usually attributed to A. S. Wilson, which beautifully conveys that sentiment:

> Not merely in the words you say,
> Not only in your deeds confessed,
> But in the most unconscious way
> Is Christ expressed.
>
> For me 'twas not the truth you taught,
> To you so clear, to me still dim,
> But when you came to me,
> You brought a sense of Him.

\*\*\*

As Grace's confinement drew near, Tom realized that he would have to deliver their baby, for there was no other doctor or midwife. It was a situation that many medical missionaries faced and none relished. As a doctor's wife in Scotland, Grace would have had every professional courtesy; in Chaoyang he could only do his best. He made copious notes in his diary, including the pros and cons of using chloroform.

All went well and Edgar was born on 21 September 1897, a big energetic baby with thick black hair. His eyes were blue at birth but soon turned black. Their Chinese friends were delighted. '*Ayee*,' they exclaimed. 'He is one of us.' Tradition had it that all foreigners were blue-eyed, big-nosed and hairy, and everybody knew that their babies were ugly little creatures.

# 5

## *Life in the villages*

Chaoyang was only a part of Tom's vast parish. He calculated that if he were to visit all the villages within a 15-mile radius of Chaoyang at the rate of one a week, it would take two years to complete the circuit. Beyond that radius James Gilmour had established a network of dressing stations in barns and abandoned buildings in villages across the plains, some of them 130 miles away. A rich evangelistic field lay there, but it was bandit territory. Travellers set out and sometimes were never seen again. More than once Tom was chased by brigands and only the strong walls of an inn saved him.

He wrote frankly in a letter soon after arriving: 'I have been opening up some new places. The policy may be right or it may be wrong. Perhaps it is dictated by ambition. But a man must have some go in him, or he'll shrink and mummify.' He rarely went on these journeys alone; he took Mister Heaven or another Chinese evangelist with him and they were away for days. They drove a pony cart through the winter floods and the summer heat. In the villages, Mister Heaven would introduce Tom as 'our doctor' with a flourish.

Most villagers had never seen a Westerner before and they were very inquisitive. Tom was intrigued by what he called 'the psychology of a first contact'. One man fingered the lapel of his coat. 'This is very fine cloth,' he said. 'How much does it cost?' Another asked his age and how many wives he had. Another said, 'You have a Queen of England, don't you? Do you know her? What will you tell her about us when you return?'

Others were suspicious and swore he was up to mischief. 'Why did you leave your home and come here? I say you are a spy. Or a merchant come to make money out of us. What's your game?' It never occurred to them that he had no ulterior motive and wanted only to do them good.

After a few visits, Mister Heaven, who watched him closely at work, suggested it would help if he dressed like a Chinese and grew a pig-tail. 'Besides,' he added, 'you are too handsome to be an *iang-ren*. God meant you to be Chinese.' When James Hudson Taylor, director of the China Inland Mission, instructed his missionaries to adopt local dress, Europeans in the treaty ports disapproved strongly; this was 'going na-tive'. Nonetheless Tom took the advice, which proved good. When he was transformed into a kindly Chinese doctor in cap and gown with a pigtail down his back, the villagers welcomed him courteously and offered him tea and sweet pancakes. In summer they set up a trestle table in the centre of the village for his equipment. The clinic was a show, like the Tibetan magicians and the gypsies with their dancing bears, and it was free.

In the villages, most of what doctors today call 'clinical events' were one-off encounters. Tom never saw the patient again and had no way of knowing the outcome. All he could do was pray that his skill and kind words made an impression and brought the name of Yeh-su (Jesus) to the families and friends of his patients. He scattered seeds of love into the strong Mongolian winds without knowing where they landed.

\*\*\*

After the villagers quietened down, Mister Heaven would start to preach. He had a gift of adapting Bible stories to a Chinese setting. Thus Noah became a lovable mandarin who brandished his silk um-brella at the first drops of rain before scuttling off to a gigantic junk. Daniel was a plucky peasant lad who confronted a fiery dragon. The crowd was spellbound and at the end of the sermon they begged for more.

Mister Heaven spoke fluent Mongolian and he would switch be-tween languages so nobody was left out. Once a herdsman at the back of the crowd stood up and tore all his clothes off. For a moment, it seemed he had gone mad, but he was suffering from scabies and had an unbearable itch.

'How long have you had it?' Mister Heaven yelled in Mongolian over the heads of the people.

'Two months,' the man yelled back.

'Well, hang on another two minutes till I finish my sermon.'

Skin diseases were common among the Mongolians, who seldom washed. There was a belief dating back to Genghis Khan that if you used too much water you became a fish in the next life. And what son of the Great Khan wanted to end up as a fish?

There were moments of hilarity. Once, exhausted by his morning clinic, Tom was resting with his hat over his eyes, his bench tilted against a wall. Beside him an old man sat snoring, his arms tucked up inside his capacious sleeves. In that attitude he nodded forward like a fallen idol, fast asleep. A small boy kicked the legs of the bench forward and trapped both men in an undignified position. Then he stuffed his family god, a live hedgehog, up the old man's trouser leg, creating uproar. A bevy of village beauties with scarlet trousers shrieked from the top of a refuse heap. Mister Heaven continued to preach in a loud voice until order was restored and the god was back in its shrine. He finished with a stern rebuke concerning 'kitchen deities'.

There was pathos too. When Tom told the peasants about Jesus, their faces went blank. Few believed that their lives could be improved and, if they did, they lacked the will to make it happen. A boy grew into a man and barely had time to sire children before he was spent. If in his short existence there was one precious hour, never to be repeated, when he heard of an extraordinary love that could turn despair into hope, how could he understand it? Tom wrote:

> My heart often bleeds to see old men and women with white hair and bleared eyes gazing stupidly into my face, unable to comprehend what all this talk means about one called Jesus. When one remembers that for two thousand years men and women like these have fallen and been swept away like autumn leaves without a single chance to hear the story of Calvary, one is overwhelmed by sorrow.

In the end Tom realized that the only people who accepted him were the poorest of the poor. Their gratitude was as deep as their needs. They were also his teachers. He was the expert, yet they knew infinitely more about pain and suffering than he did. Their courage and endurance were his tutors. Often he saw more than a hundred patients in a day and fell asleep over his supper, too tired to preach. That was frustrating, but he had Mister Heaven at his side to fill the gap. Every time a soul received Christ, the two men gave God the glory and thanked the Lord for putting them together. Tom's love for the people grew steadily.

\*\*\*

What of the Mongolian minority? As I have described, the Chinese had taken over the best land in the region, and although their tools were primitive, they usually produced good harvests. The villages were almost entirely populated by Chinese. The Mongols were uninterested in agriculture and did not raise pigs or chickens; their herds of horse, sheep, cattle and camels were all they cared about. But from time to time they quit the plains and drifted into the towns. There they intermarried with Chinese and Manchurians until it was difficult to tell the ethnic composition of a family.

Cut off from their nomadic existence, the urban Mongols lived in great poverty and for them life was a matter of survival. Their houses had no roofs and were open to sandstorms which deposited silt everywhere. A family lived in one room, crowded on the *kang*. Their fuel was dried cow dung and their food was bread made from sorghum (also a cattle food) or porridge made from millet. Occasionally they had pickled turnips. This diet made mental effort difficult and nearly all of them were illiterate. Few of them spoke Mandarin and it took a long time to teach them the basics of the Christian faith.

Syphilis was a serious threat to the Mongols and in some regions half the population was affected. Their fertility was reduced and many babies were stillborn or died young. The disease contributed heavily to Mongolian underpopulation. They accepted Tom's help but they could pay him nothing. 'We are those who are destined to feed on bitterness,' they would say. If they had any money they spent it on *airag*, alcohol made from fermented mare's milk. It took a lot to get drunk, but they were practised at it. On the other hand, they left opium to the Chinese.

All in all, it was difficult to make any headway with the Mongolians and conversions were rare. Tom wrote with rare delight in a report to London: 'At T'a Tzu Kou we have had the unique pleasure and privilege of bringing a Mongol convert into the church. His family idol makes a very fine ornament for my room.'

One ancient Mongolian tribesman was a typical case. On a day when a fair was in progress in Chaoyang, a band of nomads rode in, bringing sheep and furs to barter for salt and brass kettles. They were good customers, though the townsfolk complained that they stank. A common saying (which was also used of Russians) was, 'A nomad takes a bath a year, if he needs it.'

This old man entered the dispensary, bowing respectfully. Like most of his kind he was short and swarthy with high cheekbones. He was bent by rheumatism and his skin no longer seemed to fit him. His black eyes darted around the room, taking everything in. Was he a spy or a seeker after spiritual truth?

He had come, he said, to meet the man who had succeeded his friend, 'the worthy Gilmour', of whom he spoke warmly. Had Gilmour not shared his tent and food? Had he not learned the secrets of the Gobi and how to draw a bow? And did he not ride on short stirrups which (as everyone knew) the other *iang-ren* despised?

The old man claimed that Gilmour never preached to the Mongols. He was certain of it and wanted to know why the new doctor troubled his kinspeople with his preaching. Gilmour knew that Confucius was superior to other teachers, so why didn't he? And if this Jesus was so important, why had he not been born a Mongol – or even a Chinese?

Tom had to ride out a lecture. He was informed that a good Confucian had no sins and needed no saviour. It was an insult to call him a sinner. Of course you could say these things to the Chinese because they needed correction; they thought themselves superior to the Mongolians, which was nonsense. The Chinese did not lie as well and when they stole, they got caught. And everybody knew that if you could not do something better than your neighbour, you were simply inferior.

It became clear that the old man had not come to debate theology; he wanted something but was too proud to ask for it. Eventually Tom broached the subject of his health. Was there any service he could perform for his elder brother? After repeatedly boasting that he was in perfect health, the old man accepted a jar of eye salve.

Then came the parting shot. 'If the doctor visits me in the desert, he can share my yurt, if he can find it. But please let him not come on a camel. I have three of my own and a strange camel would not receive so generous a welcome.'

Tom was troubled by the encounter but Mister Heaven roared with laughter. He had heard this kind of nonsense many times – of course Gilmour preached to the nomads! What was more, they were Buddhists, not Confucians. The truth was that most nomads had no intention of becoming Christians. It meant leaving their family, their tribe and their herds. This rascal was teasing them and, yes, he was after free medicine.

# 6

## *The scourge of Mongolia*

The number of believers in Chaoyang grew steadily and by the end of 1898 the membership was around 200, with half as many enquirers. They gathered regularly in the chapel to hear Mister Heaven preach, but Sunday morning services were poorly attended because the Chinese did not have a day of rest and their masters would not release them. In contrast the Sunday evening service attracted up to 80 people, and the hall got so crowded that they sometimes moved out to the compound. The winds blew out the lamps, but the congregation learned the hymns and songs by heart.

What, you may ask, was Tom's own spiritual life like during this time? Did his lamp ever blow out? The diaries which he kept from an early age provide some insights, but he stopped writing at times, claiming that the frequent use of the first-person singular nauseated him. More likely, he simply lacked the time for it. Months and even years separate the entries and in later life he regretted that he had not been more conscientious. During the voyage to the East in 1897, he lost sight of what he called his 'dear old book' and was delighted to be reunited with it at Tientsin.

His diaries and day books are frank about his failings and equally harsh towards the apathy of Christians back home, particularly their lack of interest in mission. He was ashamed of some of his friends, to whom he felt Christ had been saying for years: 'Go into the world and preach the gospel to every creature.' Yet they ignored the call.

To Tom the greatest challenge facing a Christian is to understand the meaning of the word 'holy' and how to live a life that is set apart and pleasing to God. He found it far from easy to do so in China and wrote, 'I am convinced it is easier to die for Christ than to live for Him.' He would soon see that belief tested in the lives of thousands of martyrs. The anchor of his spiritual life was prayer, which in lighter moments he called 'knee drill' and at others 'my times of thunder'. Everything depended upon maintaining his prayer habit, which he described as 'a perfect hour spent each day in the presence of God'.

The habit went back to his boyhood. Before anyone else stirred in the house in Greenock, he sought out a quiet place. There he would pour out his heart, asking for grace for the day ahead, repenting of his boyish sins, praying for his family and friends, and lamenting the evil he saw in the streets. Over the years he learned what many Christians never learn: not just to cry out in prayer but to wait patiently for answers to come. He spent as much time listening to God as he did crying out to him.

Prayer moulded Tom. He grew into a man of great self-control, rarely raising his voice, and firm but fair in his judgements. When he had to confront enemies of the faith – which happened regularly in China – he did so in a way that did not demean people and instead tried to win them round. He learned the wisdom of the Chinese saying: 'If you are patient in one moment of anger, you will escape a hundred days of sorrow.'

But while he always had time for non-believers and waverers, Tom had less for Christians who did not see things his way or dragged their feet. Those who accomplish great things in God are often like that; they have an edginess that comes from firm convictions, coupled with a keen sense of urgency. In that respect they are not unlike entrepreneurs whose dynamism borders on the ruthless. Tom's blunt Scottish approach meant that he was not always popular and he was often misunderstood.

In contrast, the language of his diary is often flowery in a quaint Victorian way. 'God has sent me to unfurl His banner in the breeze,' he wrote on arriving in Mongolia, adding the word *Excelsior*. It appears frequently in his diary as a form of self-encouragement and is Latin for 'upwards' or 'ever higher'.

In his day books, he set out a daily programme which he frequently revised. So many hours were to be spent in Bible study, so many in prayer, in medical study, in language lessons and so on. During his first three years, Mandarin occupied up to seven hours a day. The London Missionary Society insisted that all its workers sat annual language examinations until they were fluent. They were organized by senior men at the regional stations.

Tom's writings also show his dismay at the hostility shown to the gospel in Chaoyang; once he had settled in, he tried to analyse the reasons behind it. First and foremost was the mindset of the population, which was a mixture of ignorance, superstition and mistrust. The Cochranes had to be careful not to do anything that might arouse suspicions. The most innocent pastime like sketching outdoors or amateur geology (even picking up coloured stones) could lead to accusations that they were using wizardry to drive away the local gods. And that could lead to a more serious charge of scooping out eyes and cutting out hearts.

Ignorance went hand in hand with illiteracy; fewer than five per cent of the urban Chinese could read or write and even fewer in the villages and among the Mongols. The missionaries argued that if converts were to retain their faith, they must be able to read the Bible. They invested a great deal of their resources in adult literacy, but even if a person lived within reach of a mission and agreed to attend for instruction, it could take years before he or she was competent.

Chinese society was also riddled with addictions. Opium pipes and bowls were as common in the homes of the nobility as in those of beggars. Everyone decried the habit but there was little shame in it. Many well-off Chinese became addicted and then lived in fear of being unable to run their business or maintain their position in society. They smoked all night and slept all day. The mandarins used opium, because (it was said) it helped them to plot and scheme their wicked ways.

The poor were the greatest losers. Opium drained a person of physical energy, and the saying ran, 'An opium smoker is not worth his food.' Two-thirds of a labourer's wages could go on the habit, and if the head of a household became addicted, his or her dependants would be reduced to begging or starvation. Opium literally destroyed families by a combination of impoverishment, starvation and early death, often by suicide. In the cities whole families died out, rich and poor. A missionary in Jiangsu province wrote, 'A friend of mine once asked a beggar who slept next door to an opium den where he lived. He replied, "Next door to hell".'

*Street beggars in their hovel*

The opium dealers and den owners could be a danger to missionaries if they felt that their livelihood was threatened. One man went around Chaoyang with a loaded gun and boasted that he would shoot Tom, but it came to nothing. Later in his career Tom came face to face with the devastating effects of opium among the slum dwellers of Peking. The Chinese called them 'opium devils' and the Europeans called them 'opium sots'. We shall see in a later chapter how Tom treated addicts.[1]

Opium was not the only addiction. Eighty per cent of men smoked or chewed tobacco and most Chinese women had a pipe permanently stuck in their mouths. Snuff taking was common among both

---

[1] See also Appendix 2 for the complexities of the international opium trade and its effects.

Mongolians and Chinese. Consumption of *airag*, wine, beer and spirits was high when there was money to pay for them, and drunkenness was common. And religion itself was an addiction.

There were other factors which kept the people in a state of nervous tension. For example, bandits were a constant menace, and not just to the missionaries when they ventured unarmed beyond the protection of a consul. The whole population feared them, and when troubles arose, victims flooded into Tom's dispensary nursing bullet wounds, sword slashes and torture burns. But at least the bandits posed no spiritual danger.

*A* yamen *or magistrates' court, 1889*

The attitude to the Christian faith among the mandarins, who were the local magistrates and administrators, varied from place to place. But their treatment of their own people was inevitably harsh. The government paid them a pittance, about the same as Tom's salary, but they rarely received it so they forced bribes out of poor people to maintain their standard of living. The *yamen* (or magistrates' court) in Chaoyang was known as 'The Court of Injustice'.

A cynical alliance existed between those who held the power. The lamas squeezed the people till the pips squeaked, and if anyone protested, he or she was arrested as a debtor by the *yamen*. Everything worked against the common man or woman: an enemy with a score to settle could bring charges without taking an oath and there were no defence lawyers. If an accused person landed in prison, the jailers could be bribed to suffocate the prisoner.

*Punishment by the* cangue, *Shangai 1870. The offender's name and crime are written on the board. The punishment is more lethal than it appears*

'The Cangue (collar of wood, punishment)' by John Thomson. Wellcome Collection. CC BY

Torture was part of Chinese 'justice', and punishments were unbelievably cruel. It is impossible to decide in retrospect whether the indifference to suffering displayed by the average Chinese was the cause or the effect of this cruelty. The contrast with their courtesy and deference to their guests and rulers seems astonishing. For example, there was a devilish invention to punish the kinds of minor offences for which the English had once used the stocks. It was the *cangue*, a French word meaning a yoke. If a man was found guilty by the *yamen*, two heavy wooden boards were locked around his neck. His crime and punishment were written on them and he was chained to a post. The subtlety of this punishment (which was frequently lethal) was that his hands were free but they could not reach his mouth and he relied on the goodness of passers-by to feed him. Without their assistance, he starved to death. Those who had profaned the gods usually died long before their sentence was up.

*Mass execution of Boxer rebels by the dreaded cage*

For a more spectacular ending – and spectacles were important to the Manchus – there was the cage. A heavy wooden structure like a giant lampshade was fixed with a halter around a prisoner's neck. Inside it he strained constantly upwards on tiptoe to relieve the pressure until, exhausted by the effort, he sank down and the halter strangled him. The process could take days, depending on the person's strength. Sometimes he was positioned on a pile of stone slabs, from which one piece was removed each day until he slipped and perished.

In *Among the Mongols* James Gilmour described a scene in a Mongolian town called Lama Miao (now known as Duolon in Chinese) in the 1870s. A man in a cage was set down before a line of eating booths where the customers mocked the poor wretch as they ate and drank. Gilmour found their heartlessness as horrifying as the man's suffering. He wrote, 'It was impossible to look on the multitude around him showing symptoms of being dead to all compassion, and not pity the hardness of their hearts.'

When it came to judicial execution, beheading was the method of choice. The Imperial Government, the European troops and the Boxers all used it. A pigtail firmly grasped and stretched towards the swordsman made decapitation easy. The method appealed particularly to the foreign soldiers, and hundreds of photographs were taken of summary beheadings in the ruins of Peking. Normally executions took place on a busy thoroughfare or a street corner. By the time they were three years of age, children were hardened to these sights.

Prisoners and convicts were one section of the community that Tom could never reach, though he tried repeatedly. For three years he treated the blind and preached the good news to the poor, but he was never permitted into the Chaoyang jail, where 35 prisoners languished in a cell 12 feet square. The mandarins regarded Tom as 'a nail in the eye', a Chinese way of describing someone who is a great nuisance.

As far as the London Missionary Society was concerned, prisoners were not part of Tom's remit and members of the Board may not have appreciated the true savagery of Chinese justice. He decided to enlighten them with an eyewitness report which spared no details. In it he described the wretched victims leaving the prison house too dazed to realize what was happening. They huddled together in an open cart and were driven through crowded streets to a sandy depression in a treeless plain.

> Here, in presence of a multitude of spectators who stand on the high ground, they kneel in a row. The assistant grasps the pigtail and pulls upon it to stretch their neck and then the executioner with his sword does what the Chinese think is a dreadful thing, he sends them into the next world without a head.

The executioners stuck the heads on the town walls or hung them in baskets at street corners. Worse was to follow. To increase the sense of shame, the bodies were left unburied for wild dogs and pigs to eat and the sights were past description. Sometimes the native doctors bought the remains. Bread saturated with the blood of decapitated prisoners was sold as a remedy for indigestion. Heads were boiled into a concoction to make men brave and bones were ground into a powder to control haemorrhage. (A faint note in Tom's handwriting in the margin of his journal adds, 'Flesh . . . per lb, sold, dear'.)[2] Nevertheless, the crime rate never varied, which suggests that these horrors were at best a weak deterrent. Familiarity bred contempt for the law.

After his visits to the execution ground, Grace would find her husband sitting on the bed, his head in his hands. 'Don't take it on yourself, Tom,' she would say. 'It's not your business and they're wicked men.' Maybe she was right, but who were more wicked, the prisoners or their executioners? Tom could not get the horrors out of his head and he could not find a solution. All he could do was to get on his knees and pray.

\*\*\*

The other great scourge of Mongolia was religion. Most of the population practised what was called 'the great religion', a mixture of Buddhism, Confucianism, Taoism and shamanism. The Mongolians were devoted to sorcery and fortune telling. The brand of Buddhism practised in north China was called the 'Yellow Hat religion', a sect of Tibetan Buddhism that had been expelled from Tibet. Mildred Cable (1878–1952), a missionary with the China Inland Mission, witnessed it first-hand in Tibet. She wrote, 'The sense of the presence of evil is beyond anything known in England. I have never felt

---

[2] These gruesome practices owed something to the funeral habits of the Mongols. On the plains there were no cemeteries; bodies were laid out for vultures and wolves to devour. (This is the 'sky funeral' which persists today.) The speed with which the body vanished was a measure of the deceased's virtue. After three days the lamas collected the leftovers. Femurs were fashioned into trumpets to keep evil spirits at bay and skulls were covered with animal skins to make drums. Some were covered with silver to make ceremonial mugs.

it in China as I have felt it in Tibet, in places where Satan seems to have his seat.'

As the sect spread across Mongolia, its priests established a lamasery (monastery) in every district and each became the nucleus of a town. Soon the lamas owned half the cattle and the land. They imposed heavy taxes on agricultural produce and on pilgrims journeying to the Four Sacred Mountains of Wutai. Devotees covered every yard of the way with their bodies, lying down and making a mark in the dust with their heads before scrambling up and bringing their feet to the mark, then lying down again. In this way a pilgrimage could occupy three years of a person's life. John Gilmour wrote about a man who travelled a hundred miles on his belly, kowtowing at every shrine and banging his forehead until a fibrous lump grew out of it like a turnip. He also wrote of a boy who crawled from one temple to another with a saddle on his back and a skewer thrust through his flesh, crying out 'For my mother's sake'.

There was no consolation to be had from the lamas, for they were illiterate and did no teaching or preaching. Nor could they speak Tibetan, so the prayers and the rituals they mumbled were as meaningless to them as to anyone else. They took a vow of celibacy, but the lamaseries were rife with homosexuality and since the monks made up 60 per cent of the male population, entire regions were in danger of underpopulation.

For all its failings, the Yellow Hat religion exercised enormous power. James Gilmour noted that the average Mongolian was constantly counting beads, saying prayers and doing the rounds of the shrines. He wrote:

> There is scarcely one single step in life, however insignificant, which can be taken [by a Mongolian] without first consulting his religion through his priest. It would be difficult to find another instance in which any religion has grasped a country so universally and completely as Buddhism has Mongolia.

Whenever Tom visited the Longxiang temple in Chaoyang, he was surprised that such an imposing building and so many priests could be supported by such a poor and thinly spread population. Whenever he tried to talk to the priests, his words were lost in the whirring of prayer wheels and the flutter of prayer flags. Thousands of these brightly decorated cylinders adorned the temple. They contained prayers written on paper slips: 'May my neighbour take sick and die', 'May my husband love me again', 'May evil spirits leave my daughter', and so on. The idea was that spinning the cylinder had the same spiritual effect as if you had prayed all those prayers, and if you spun it long enough they would be answered. In some temples a large cylinder contained books as well as prayers. If a person spun it long enough he or she acquired all the knowledge in the book. Needless to say, this appealed to the illiterate populace.

In the monasteries the lamas found a clever way of fixing their prayer wheels in a draught so that they spun unaided. That way they accumulated virtue whether they were awake or asleep. Prayer was no longer spiritual but mechanical. Tom was always glad to leave the temple because he felt a strong sense of evil. Mister Heaven said he was not surprised – everyone knew the lamas practised demon worship.

\*\*\*

Once the head lama visited the dispensary in person. He was like a hunched yellow stork in his saffron robes and coxcomb hat which made him tower over his attendants. His hooded eyes bored into Tom and his voice rasped like parchment. 'I have certain symptoms,' he said. The attendants stroked the air with giant fans and shooed away the flies while their master described his digestive symptoms. Tom gave him a prescription and some instructions. A week later the lama returned, complaining of other symptoms. Tom explained they were sometimes a consequence of the medicine he had been given. Perhaps His Reverence had taken all the pills at once?

The old man's lip curled as he rubbed his spectacles on his sleeve. Could the clever doctor not tell? No, he had not taken any of the foreign medicine. The attendants sniggered. It was a trick, of course, to humiliate Tom and make him lose face. The lama had hoodwinked Liu-i into telling him what side effects went with an overdose. The man would stop at nothing to discredit a foreigner.

If Lamaism was the most corrupt of faiths, Taoism was the most superstitious. It created a labyrinthine world in which demon spirits and gods lurked behind every boulder. Every home had a household god which lived in a shrine and had be tended and revered. These beings had no moral sense and they turned very nasty if offended. The whole system was based on fear; in times of trouble the populace crowded into the Taoist temples to appease the gods.

Confucianism in contrast was perhaps the loftiest moral code ever devised, apart from the teachings of Jesus Christ. Though clear and beautiful in its intentions, it did not include belief in either a deity or an afterlife: as a moral compass it lacked a true north. Although the emperors professed for centuries to exemplify Confucius' teachings, the ethos of government sadly remained corrupt, cruel and disdainful towards life.

Whatever faith the Chinese professed, they all observed the cult of what the missionaries called 'ancestor worship'. This was a matter of honour and tradition from the richest to the poorest families. The 'worship' seems to have been mainly an excessive care and reverence for the memory, spirits and graves of ancestors. Every home contained a shrine for the ancestral tablets, one tablet per ancestor, going back several generations. The tablets were also the resting place of their souls and were themselves to be worshipped. In addition, a book recorded the names of the generations who had passed on. Their spirits watched over the family and it was the sacred duty of the eldest son to take care of them.

But with this excessive reverence, the Chinese instruction to 'treat death as life' became a licence for extortion. It required elaborate funeral ceremonies and constant care of the graves so that they would never fall into decay or be lost. As a result, Chinese cemeteries were vast in size. In some districts they seriously reduced the amount of arable land.

When someone died, diviners, musicians and priests were called in to perform rites which lasted for weeks. Mirrors were covered over and everything coloured red was put away. The family members gathered in mourning clothes and kept night vigils; the priests prayed and chanted Buddhist scriptures; the diviners made horoscopes; the musicians beat drums and gongs, and the feasting lasted for days. Objects made out of *papier mâché* and wood were prepared for the dead person's use. If he or she was wealthy they included a house, a horse, a cart, servants, cattle and food. Money was placed in the coffin, and a jewel in the corpse's mouth. On the burial day all these objects, including the paper money, were burned. A cake containing a mass of hairs was placed in the coffin to throw to the dogs that guarded the spirit world. The idea was that if they refused to admit the dead person, they would choke on a massive hairball.

A good funeral put a family in debt for years. After the mourning was over, the relatives continued to bring offerings of food and money to the graveside. On holidays and at festivals, they invited the dead to join them. They gave them all the village news and showed off any new babies that had arrived. If any detail was omitted, bad luck and accidents would follow, so the bereaved lived in constant fear of putting a foot wrong. Nonetheless they clung stubbornly to their comfortless beliefs.

The eldest son was charged with placating the guardians of the underworld on behalf of his parents. If he did not tend their graves and leave money and food, they wandered as hungry ghosts in the afterlife. This, of course, made it imperative for every man to have a son to carry on the rites. Daughters were no use; they would marry and worship the spirits of their in-laws. As a result, female babies were regarded as of little value, with tragic consequences. Female infanticide was widespread throughout rural China.

The implications for missionaries were enormous. For a young Chinese man to show an interest in following Jesus or even to consider attending a church was a serious matter for the whole community. It challenged every convention and belief it held dear. It brought him endless problems with his family, his friends and his employer. Tom described a father prostrating himself before his son, imploring him to give up the foreign god: 'Do you wish to see your poor parents naked and starving in the next world?' He added, 'It is not to be wondered at if sons are threatened with torture and death unless they recant.'

\*\*\*

How did Grace Cochrane fare in Chaoyang? Unfortunately, little personal information about her survives and I have seen only two photographs. She was like many women whose lives are dedicated to their families and whose identities merge with those of others, particularly their husbands. But she played a critical part in keeping the family safe and together. Years later her son Robert wrote:

> It was she who, in days of danger and peril – peril through climate,
> peril through disease, and peril from bandits – shared my father's life.
> It was she who, in later years, during the intervals when the head of the
> family was away, kept the lamp of faith burning bright at the family
> altar. There was incident after incident which could have ended in
> death or worse, but for the good hand of the Lord upon the family.

There was a great deal for Grace and Tom to pray about in Chaoyang, together and individually. Practical problems loomed large
and Tom found himself rising earlier and earlier to go to his place of
thunder. One seemingly small but important problem was the dispensary waiting room, which was always crowded. Men and women
were forced to sit together, which was against Chinese custom. It
also interfered with Mister Heaven's teaching. When the room filled
up in winter, the patients huddled in the compound at the mercy of
the weather. Some of them developed frostbite before they could be
seen.

The London Missionary Society sent no money for buildings and
Tom decided to introduce small charges for medicines but not for
treatment, and only for those who could afford them. The poorest
patients he continued to supply free. It was not an easy decision and
he knew it would be unpopular. But Tom always believed that (in his
own words) 'independence is precious', whether it was a patient con-
tributing towards his or her treatment, or a missionary planting an
indigenous church. He longed for the converts in Chaoyang to make a
proper commitment to their new faith:

> The sooner that people understand that embracing the Christian reli-
> gion means giving as well as getting, the better. If a man is not willing
> to spend as much on the worship of the true God as he formerly did
> on heathen rites, we will have a right at least to question the soundness
> of his conversion!

Nonetheless Tom was optimistic about the money: 'I am only creeping
at present but soon I hope to be walking. If I should have a peaceful
year and can manage to get our hospital accommodation provided, I
am confident of the results financially.'

\*\*\*

Behind all Tom's concern with the difficulties to hand, I believe there lay a deeper question. He wrote in his diary, 'My Father, I have several difficulties and one is to know what thoughts are legitimate and what are not.' What did he mean? I suspect that early on in Chaoyang, Tom felt that he was being wasted. He might stay for 10 or 20 years, but he questioned what his skills and sacrifice would achieve. A few lives saved, a few lives bettered, a few converts made – that was all. He had come to Mongolia believing that modern medicine was one key to awakening the people to the love of Jesus, though he never placed their physical before their spiritual well-being. But when he tried to talk to his patients about Jesus, the answer was often, 'Thank you, *tai-fu*, but I have my own gods to pray to. I don't need another.' How naive to think that Mongolia could be won in a decade!

Much of the time his medical practice kept him physically exhausted. He fell into the trap that awaits all highly motivated clinicians under pressure: working longer and longer hours. Their health and well-being suffer, but their experience and usefulness grow. Tom was so much in demand that he had little time to preach the gospel.

Like a good wife, Grace kept telling him there was no point in killing himself and that patients would always come back the next day; whatever he did was a drop in the torrent of their suffering. She was right. Tom estimated that across the Chinese Empire, 40,000 men and women perished every day, many of them suffering painful and avoidable deaths. The death rate was like the Yangtze River in spate; you might pluck an occasional soul to safety but in so doing you missed a hundred others. And all the time the river rose higher.

There had to be a better way to use his training and his skills. And so Tom's dream was born, on a beaten mud floor with women squatting on their heels, babies wailing and tuberculous peasants coughing up their souls. In those surroundings it could not have seemed less attainable. It was to build a medical college and a teaching hospital, with facilities equal to the best in Britain or America. It would have a dedicated teaching staff and a scientific curriculum, taught in Chinese to Chinese students. Its medical degrees would be approved by the Imperial Government. At the same time – and this was essential – the students would receive instruction in the Christian faith.

A wild notion, far ahead of its time? Perhaps so, but so was Tom's decision to become a doctor and a missionary. You could also look on it as a step of faith and one that made sense. The reason for Mister Heaven's effectiveness as a preacher was that he knew how the Chinese mind worked and he foresaw obstacles which never occurred to a European. In the same way Liu-i, Tom's apprentice, understood how their ignorance and superstitions affected their health. He would make an excellent doctor, whereas a European would always be at a disadvantage in China.

There was only one place to locate such a college. Peking was tucked away in the north-east corner of China but it was the administrative and educational heart, and well connected by railways, telegraph, sea and canals. Thousands of students flocked there every year. Its citizens spoke the best Mandarin in China (so they claimed), which was widely spoken through the north. And the timing was right for a bold endeavour; the Imperial Board of Education was following the example of Germany and Japan, trying to impose uniform policies across the nation.

In passing, one must admit that Tom's idea was not new. Medical missionaries invariably try to pass on their knowledge to others, and they did so particularly in China. Unlike India, China had no government medical schools and its needs were limitless. Starting with Dr Peter Parker, the American Presbyterian in Canton in the 1830s, missionaries taught male Chinese orderlies how to change dressings, prepare and dispense drugs, and treat minor injuries. These apprentices were expected to become assistants and aides to the Western doctors, but in a limited way.

In some hospitals – the few which had two or more doctors – the training developed into 'schools' of a primitive kind.[3] The missionaries

---

[3] Today the pioneer work of these medical teachers is largely forgotten. They include Peter Parker, Benjamin Hobson and John Kerr in Canton, and Percy McCall and Tom Gillison of the London Missionary Society in Hankow. In Tientsin, Kenneth Mackenzie (also of the LMS) opened a primitive school in 1881. In Mukden (Shenyang) Dugald Christie, a Scottish Presbyterian, opened another in 1892; it evolved into the Mukden Medical College in 1912. The first school for women students opened in Soochow in 1891. On the island of Hong Kong a medical college dated from 1887, but that was in a crown colony directly administered by the British.

had little time for teaching and there were few medical texts, but they did their best. With no academic experience except their own undergraduate years, they had to work out a curriculum on an *ad hoc* basis. There was no standardization or external supervision. Above all there was no recognition by the Imperial Government. Any examinations, diplomas or certificates had only local value. The students were taught little of the scientific basis of medicine, but that did not stop the bright ones (like Li Hsiao Ch'uan in Peking whom we shall meet later) from becoming competent clinicians. Most of them stayed in missionary service, but occasionally they left and set up as Western-trained doctors.

Tom's dream was on a far greater scale. It was a purpose-made college run by medical missionaries alongside a modern teaching hospital that would produce a steady stream of medical graduates. They would gain degrees approved by the Imperial Board of Education that were equal to any British or American degree. They would become leaders of their profession, working in cities, towns and villages throughout China, in hospitals, dispensaries, government service and the armed forces. Achieving all this would need not one but a series of miracles. Meanwhile an old Chinese saying ran, 'One seeing is worth a thousand hearings.' Tom resolved to teach Liu-i as much clinical medicine as possible, and in his remaining time to turn the lad into a competent assistant. His remaining time? Yes, Tom did not know it but his days in Mongolia were numbered.

# 7

## *The gathering storm*

As the nineteenth century drew to a close, the economic and political pressures inside China came to a head like lava forcing its way through rock. It erupted at the weakest point, the north-east. Disaster took the form of a series of alternating droughts and floods. The great northern plain that lies between Peking and the Yangtze River is an area of 8,000 square miles. It was intensively farmed and supported a large population by agriculture alone. Every square foot of earth was taken up by cereal crops, fertilized by human excrement. The landscape at that time was devoid of trees and shrubs and it was a mystery how the carters navigated across the network of tracks without landmarks.

Everything on the great plain operated at subsistence level; if a flood washed away a harvest or the sun scorched it to death, there was no grain left for the next year's planting. The plain was at the limit of the Asian monsoons so the rains often failed and the people were accustomed to drought. Between 1876 and 1879 a continuous drought devastated five provinces and left between 9 and 13 million dead. In Shanxi province a Welsh missionary, the Revd Timothy Richard, described apocalyptic scenes. Desperate men sold their wives and daughters into prostitution and people devoured roots and carrion. Babies were boiled and eaten. And because the drought had no logical explanation, it was attributed to the wrath of the gods and that in turn was attributed to the foreigners. At the time, there were no Protestant missionaries stationed in the famine-stricken districts so there were no anti-missionary incidents.

In 1887 there was a different kind of calamity. The Yellow River, known as 'China's Sorrow', broke its levees and caused the second deadliest flooding in history; nearly a million peasants drowned and two million were made homeless. Severe flooding occurred again between 1896 and 1898, and the Yangtze River also flooded in 1t898. Refugees poured into the towns and cities, especially in Shantung province. The survivors scavenged desperately for anything that could be eaten. In 1899 the drought returned. It hit a wider area than the floods and inflicted even greater harm. The price of grain soared. Droughts and floods did more than create famine; they turned inoffensive peasants who would otherwise be working in the fields into idlers and ne'er-do-wells who hung around the village streets full of resentment, demanding compensation from their landlords. Many moved to the towns to survive. Others turned to highway robbery and ransom. Each week of drought made the situation worse.

In 1898 food reached famine prices and unrest grew. A large number of hungry bandits poured into the Chaoyang district to plunder and burn. The soldiers attached to the *yamen* were poorly trained and no match for them. The desperadoes were better armed and better marksmen. They paraded insolently on their ponies, within rifle shot of the town walls.

Tom wrote, 'Chaoyang has a reputation for rebellious outbreaks, and at present the officials seem to be doing everything that is calculated to foster discontent.' He railed at their apathy and excuses. Placards posted secretly in the town denounced the officials as incompetent. The truth (Tom later discovered) was even more shocking. The bandits were bribing minor officials in the *yamen* to turn a blind eye and the rascals shared the money with their superiors.

In July a reign of terror began and lasted for three months. Tom recorded details in his annual report for 1898. Individuals rumoured to have money were tied up, and if they refused to pay a ransom they were scraped with iron spikes and salt was rubbed in their wounds. Others had their ears or eyelids sliced off and sent to their families with a demand for money. If it was slow in coming, other bits of anatomy followed. When the bandits ran out of patience, they poured boiling water over their victims or roasted them over a slow fire. The cruelties practised on women were so vile that Tom would not describe them.

He needed a place of safety for his own family, but all the carts had been commandeered. Carts that normally carried two or three people were leaving the town laden with a dozen women and children. After a week of confusion, the gates closed in the middle of the day, leaving the mission unprotected. Before anyone knew what was happening, a gang of mounted bandits burst into the compound. They waved their swords and screamed abuse.

The leader bristled with knives and wore half-armour over a quilted jacket. He spotted Tom standing by the dispensary door, with Grace holding her baby. He told them they were in luck. His warriors were in a generous mood and would let them live for a thousand 'taels' of silver. That was a substantial ransom, about £15,000 by today's values.

Tom spoke in the quiet courteous tone that he used in difficult circumstances. He had to disappoint His Excellency. They had no silver and nothing of value in their humble house. Lien-yi courageously joined in, saying that the doctor was poor and everything he did was without reward.

The man spat in the dust. Everyone knew the foreigners had money. He gave them two days to collect silver before they came back and extracted it by torture. Then they galloped off.

Grace was horrified. As a nurse in Glasgow she had treated victims of violence from the Gorbals, but she had never been threatened. She clutched her baby through the night. They barricaded the compound and the door of the bungalow, knowing it would not keep the bandits out for long if they returned. They pleaded with God to deliver them and show them what to do. Tom read Psalm 91, which starts:

> He that dwelleth in the secret place of the most High shall abide under the shadow of the Almighty. I will say of the LORD, He is my refuge and my fortress: my God; in him will I trust.

There was little sleep for the Cochranes that night.

The following day their prayers were answered. More troops suddenly arrived in Chaoyang. They had been requested weeks earlier but because of an administrative fault they had been delayed. The town gates opened to welcome them. Nevertheless tension remained high and Tom managed to get his family away for some weeks until things settled. This terrifying episode was a foretaste of what was to come in the Boxer Uprising. Meanwhile Tom made fewer excursions on to the plains. He had other concerns; before 1898 was out Grace discovered that she was pregnant again.

\*\*\*

That autumn the Board finally accepted that Tom needed help with his growing congregation. In spite of all the difficulties, the number of believers in Chaoyang and the villages had now grown to 350. It sent him Reverend James Liddell, who came without the young lady to whom he had been engaged for six years. The Society's policy towards a missionary who was engaged to be married was not exactly charitable; he had to pass his first language examination before his bride joined him. (I cannot think how the Cochranes managed to get around this regulation.) James Liddell's fiancée Mary Shedding came out from England in September 1899 and the couple were married in Shanghai Cathedral on 23 October. The next day they boarded a steamer for Tientsin.

Liddell was a Congregationalist minister of Tom's age and like him hailed from Greenock, so they had much in common. There was only one small house in the compound and the accommodation was cramped, but they settled in happily. Tom privately described James as 'a very promising colleague'. James Liddell wrote rather more enthusiastically, 'I do not know that I could have a more brotherly colleague than Doctor C. I have a great deal of admiration for the doctor and his wife and feel blessed in having them both as neighbours and colleagues.'

Liddell took over the evangelism programme and the services, and he held Bible classes for converts and prepared them for baptism. When Mary joined him, the two families formed a little community at the Chaoyang mission that declared love and peace in the face of hatred and tumult.

\*\*\*

The summer of 1899 was hot and dry and the bandits were again active. Tom had a narrow escape on the plains when they chased and nearly caught his cart. Mercifully there was an inn nearby, and its walls protected him and other terrified travellers.

The hills around Chaoyang shimmered in the heat as Tom began a routine antenatal check in his examination room, methodically going through one point after another. Halfway through the procedure he put down the foetal stethoscope, frowned and started again. Grace noticed and asked if everything was all right. He smiled. He could hear two foetal hearts. They were going to have twins.

In Tientsin Dr Lillie Saville, a Belgian-trained doctor with the London Missionary Society, learned the news and volunteered her obstetric skills for what might be a difficult delivery. The offer came just in time for them to leave the mission in James Liddell's hands and to make the long journey to Pei Tai Ho, affectionately known as PTH, a quiet fishing village on the Gulf of Bohai. It had recently been 'discovered' by the Europeans, who built holiday homes there. They ranged from the modest bungalows of the missionary societies to the luxury villas of the European 'taipans' – the wealthy merchants and diplomats. Every summer they flocked there to escape the heat and enjoy tennis and concert parties in relative freedom and safety. The missionaries even organized Bible conferences with speakers such as Dr F. B. Meyer from England. Today Pei Tai Ho is the busy coastal resort of Beidaihe.

Robert and Thomas were born on 11 August. They had feeding problems so the Cochranes extended their stay, and the extra time at the seaside did wonders for Grace. After the heat of Chaoyang, she loved the cool breezes and the lush vegetation. When she was strong enough, she took walks along a cliff path marked by stone seats and ornamental bridges, while Tom played with Edgar on the beach. If Tom had said they were not going back to Chaoyang, Grace would not have minded a bit. If she had known what lay in store, nothing on earth would have dragged her back.

A letter from James Liddell told them that order had been restored in Chaoyang by a troop of soldiers. A hundred bandits had been executed and the rest had fled north into the steppes. But when the family got home after the long break, the atmosphere in the town had changed. The hecklers who followed Tom around multiplied. They no longer whispered behind his back but taunted him openly: 'Oh, you're still preaching? It won't be for much longer.'

To their dismay, the missionaries stood accused of causing the drought. This became evident soon after James Liddell had christened the twins. Grace was showing them off to some women who were intrigued by their eyes. Robert and Thomas had blue eyes while Edgar's were black. A youth began to chant a rhyme: '*Yen fa lan, ti fa kan.*' Not long before, the matrons would have boxed his ears and sent him off. Now they shuffled their feet and looked down in embarrassment.

Tom explained that it was a slogan that the agitators had adopted. It meant 'Their eyes are blue, hence the earth lacks dew.' In other words, people with blue eyes were causing the drought. It shook them both. What had they brought their babies back to?

\*\*\*

On the last day of 1899, the Revd Sidney Brooks, a young Anglican missionary, was returning to his post in Pingyin in Shantung province in the snow. By misfortune he ran into a gang of local thugs who beheaded him. It was the first such outrage against a Westerner in two years and it sent a shudder through the missionary community.

In Hsiao Chang in Chihli (Zhili) province, 230 miles south of Peking, Dr Sewell McFarlane ran a mission hospital. He found scores of believers flying to him for protection from the Boxers (see pp. xix–xxii). 'We have never experienced anything like this in our twelve years' residence here,' he reported. He appealed for official protection and the government in Peking sent a detachment of troops, but it could not protect all the missionaries in the north. On New Year's Day, families in Britain celebrated the start of a new century and another year in Queen Victoria's long reign. It was a poignant time for expatriates around the world. In Chaoyang, thousands of Chinese prepared to celebrate the Year of the Metal Rat with lantern processions and dragon dances. From their bungalow the Cochranes heard firecrackers and gongs being used to ward off the evil spirits. The Zodiac sign of the rat seemed appropriate for the Boxers. The rat symbolizes a person of strong emotions and determination who is also cunning and ruthless.

As the winter passed into spring, the Christians prayed earnestly for early rains and a good harvest, but it was not to be. The rains failed entirely and the ground was so hard, it was impossible to press the seeds into it. Now it was rain processions which disturbed their sleep. These affairs were very different from the New Year festivities and full of menace. Crowds howled and screamed as they beseeched their idols to have mercy and send rain. The torchlight processions ended at a shrine where sacrifices and inflammatory speeches were made. Missionaries declared the meetings idolatrous and forbade their converts to attend. It was very dangerous to be outside at such times.

Nevertheless the work of the mission went on. From time to time Tom travelled across country to exchange paper money for lump silver. Back in Chaoyang the silver was cut up, weighed and exchanged for round copper coins with a square hole in the centre. The coin was called a *cash*, hence the English word. Often a *cash* wore so thin that it was more hole than metal.

Whenever Tom travelled he threaded the coins on a cord around his waist. Two coins paid for a night at a Chinese inn. Even that was an extortionate amount for the sordid refuge that lay across his route home on this occasion, but he was tired and hungry. He took off his boots and sat on the *kang* waiting for his supper, his eyes watering from the smoke. The place stank of urine, noodles and cooking fat.

His heavy bag had not gone unnoticed. In the next-door room two men settled down to a meal of bread and noodle soup; he heard sucking noises as they lifted the bowls to their lips. Years later he remembered the drift of their conversation.

'*Ayee.* There is a foreign devil in the inn.'

'Yes, I saw him. He has black eyes and a pigtail. He could be a Han.'

'Never. He has the milky smell of the devils. It's the reason they bathe so often.'

'No matter, the Emperor will soon get rid of them.'

'Why wait? Let's start by strangling this one and seeing what's in that bag.'

They had no idea they were overheard by a fluent Chinese speaker as they discussed their chances. Tom tiptoed out and drove for some miles to a gully, where he spent the night shivering in his cart. It was his third close shave with death, and he thanked God for deliverance.

\*\*\*

As storm clouds gathered, the Cochranes and the Liddells remained strangely ignorant of how bad things were outside Chaoyang. That was probably because of the remoteness of the town and the insulating effect of the mountains and hills. Tom had lived so long with sporadic outbreaks of violence that he did not see the major event ahead. Afterwards he wrote, 'We were not much in touch with the world outside. The Boxers seemed but a cloud the size of a man's hand, and most unlikely to overspread the whole sky.'

Besides, he had other things on his mind. In the spring of 1900 he was taking examinations. On 18 March he wrote, 'I am anxious, in spite of all the drawbacks which have threatened to thwart my endeavours, to pass my language exams in three years and I am grateful I have managed it.' 'It' was an important milestone. He did well in his second examination, achieving an overall 92 per cent and 100 per cent in Chinese characters. The examiner predicted that he would soon be fluent in idiomatic Chinese.

After three years Tom was in a sober mood. He was frustrated as a missionary as well as a doctor. He had seen the mistakes that missionary societies in China made when they introduced Western practices. He had developed a philosophy of establishing churches that were Chinese in character and financially self-supporting. Now he was asking himself how to measure success in the mission field. Could he trace all those who had professed an interest in the gospel in Chaoyang and find out what had happened to them? He was wondering, too, whether to invite his friends at home to support him financially, so as to relieve the LMS of the burden. Above all, as we have seen, he was questioning the value of his work as a clinician in Chaoyang. Another call was occupying his prayers.

In fact the Chaoyang mission had achieved a lot, thanks to the labours of the three Chinese evangelists and of James Parker, as well as of the Cochranes. Every week church services were conducted, classes for enquirers were held and children were taught in the mission school. Baptismal candidates were catechized, the illiterate were taught reading and writing, gospel meetings were held in the villages, and elders and deacons were trained. The mission also employed several *colporteurs* who distributed Bibles and tracts in the villages and at fairs and markets.

In spite of his doubts, Tom seems to have stayed mentally committed to the work in Chaoyang. Even at this late moment he wrote, 'I want to see in how many villages in this vast territory I can light a candle towards the evangelization of the world in this generation.' He dreamed of winning 150 souls a year and preaching to a church a thousand strong before he left. When a local convert announced he had personally won a hundred Christians to Christ, there was general excitement. But the man exaggerated (to put it politely), because at the end of three years the mission only had 350 converts who were divided between four locations.

As late as 1 April 1900, Tom described a successful visit to an old woman in a village called Yu Chia Wop'u. When the villagers heard he was coming, they turned it into a free-for-all in her house to show off their ailments. Old women hobbled into the room with their hands tucked up their sleeves, smoking long pipes. The air reeked of tobacco and garlic and there was a continuous refrain of coughing and spitting. The women crowded on to the *kang*, and the men and children filled the rest of the room.

When Mister Heaven began to preach, one woman who had finished her pipe punched her belly repeatedly to let the wind out. Meanwhile the elderly householder, delighted to be the focus of attention, would not stop singing a ditty in praise of the doctor. Finally Mister Heaven got tired of the hubbub and roared, 'Will you please be quiet! There's very little wrong with any of you – and whatever is wrong will be cured for certain after I have finished.'

This was greeted by clapping and laughter. Several villagers showed an interest in the gospel and said they would come to the mission station. So perhaps Tom could be forgiven for being blind to the storm that was about to break. Many were taken by surprise, and even the British minister in Peking believed that the danger from the Boxers was receding.

\*\*\*

Traditionally the *nongmin* (the Chinese word for peasants) were amazingly stoical in the face of natural disasters. They accepted flood, fire, drought and earthquakes with equal resignation and determination to survive. They did not complain when their own rulers were incompetent and indifferent to their sufferings. What was the point, when the gods directed these things?

But in 1900 they had someone to blame. In the temples and shrines across the north the priests poured fuel on the flames, accusing Christians of insulting the gods by declaring them false. They accused them of poisoning the wells, of employing magical powers and of marking doors with mystical signs that brought an angel of death upon the occupants. If the gods were to be persuaded to open the heavens and release the rain, foreign blood must be shed. A popular chant ran:

> See, the rain does not come,
> The sky is as brass.
> Foreign blood must be spilt,
> Or the season will pass.

That left two questions unanswered: how much blood and how soon?

# 8

## *'Kill the foreigners before breakfast'*

———•◆•———

By the end of May 1900, the situation in Chaoyang was deteriorating rapidly. Mongolian families, who were always sensitive to the mood changes of their Chinese neighbours, were returning to the steppes. Catholic converts were arming themselves with swords and knives. Two Europeans, managers of a gold mine, stopped briefly in the town to buy supplies. Their employers had ordered them to pull out.

Four hundred miles away in the town of Kalgan (modern Zhangjiaou) a resourceful Swedish missionary called Frans Larson heard Boxers screaming in the streets for the blood of foreigners. He happened to be preparing for a geological expedition and had already hired his pack animals, so he was able to take immediate action. He gathered 17 European adults and six children together and led them 600 miles across the plains to the safety of Ulaanbaatar, Mongolia's capital.[1]

In central and southern China rioting and persecution were sporadic, but in the provinces of Chihli, Shanxi, Shantung, Honan, Manchuria and the southern parts of Mongolia, a reign of terror was unleashed. The Boxers' battle cry was 'Kill the foreigners! Kill them before breakfast.'

Tom was not as well placed as Frans Larson. Cut off from the rest of the country in Chaoyang, he and others believed that another war with Japan had broken out. When he finally managed to contact his parent station in Tientsin, he learned for the first time how widespread the Boxer disturbances were. He was instructed to abandon the station immediately and make for the coast with both families. A

---

[1] Like James Gilmour, Larson lived among the Mongols and adopted their ways. He formed strong friendships and was given the rank of duke by one of their princes. But after 35 years in Mongolia (1893–1928) he found the Mongols no easier to convert than Gilmour did.

new railway line was being built north from Jinzhou to carry coal. If they could reach it, they would be within three days of a port. But to get there they had to cross 60 miles of country patrolled by the Boxers.

Probably out of concern for Mary Liddell, who was heavily pregnant, Tom hesitated. He asked members of his congregation to find out what they could at the *yamen*. They reported that the military governor had invited Boxer activists into the town to teach Boxer drills to the garrison. A special drill ground had been laid out where classes were held by moonlight. Tom lodged a protest, but the next thing he heard was that the Boxers were drilling by day as well as night.

The noose was tightening. A spy appeared in the compound, asking how many converts the missionaries had made and where they were meeting, but he was detected and turned away. Then Tom heard a rumour – which proved to be true – that the Empress Dowager intended to hand the foreigners over to their enemies for slaughter. An edict was being drawn up to remove official protection.

It was a great shock because, under the treaty regulations of 1860, the safety of foreigners was guaranteed by the Imperial Government. As a last resort they could surrender their passports to the local mandarin and put themselves under his protection. Mercifully Tom and James Liddell did not take this step – it had lethal consequences in other towns – but they were considering it when soldiers from the garrison suddenly arrived at the bungalow.

'By order of the *yamen*,' yelled the sergeant, slapping a paper on the table. The chief mandarin alleged that Tom was concealing ten Mauser rifles and ordered him to produce them for inspection. If they proved better than the mandarin's own arsenal, they would be requisitioned.

The allegation was preposterous of course, but Tom answered respectfully. After three years he had learned much about Chinese thinking and it was important for the sergeant not to lose face. He replied that all the people in the house were Christians and led peaceable lives. Their God taught them to love their enemies, not to shoot them. Would the good sergeant please tell the mandarin that he was misinformed and that there were no guns?

The soldiers scowled and departed, leaving the missionaries to wonder if they would be attacked immediately, now it was known they had no weapons. Had the *yamen* turned against them? Perhaps not, but even if the mandarin wanted to protect them, he might not be able. Clearly there was no help coming from Peking. They had only God's protection.

\*\*\*

In the final 24 hours stories came in which were so terrible that Tom and James Liddell kept them from their wives. On 9 June members of their own congregation were attacked and wounded, though none was killed. In the compound the missionaries abandoned the day's programme and barricaded themselves in. It was clear that Tom's delay had put them all in great danger. After discussion and prayer, they decided to get the women and children away by night. They would make for the Jinzhou railhead. James Liddell would escort them there, rally whatever armed help he could and return to Chaoyang. Grace pleaded desperately for Tom to come with them, but he insisted that he had to protect the congregation, that his presence at the mission would prevent more violence. After a long and emotional discussion he got his way, but the plan nearly failed for lack of transport. Most of the carts in the town had been commandeered and the main supplier (who was not a Christian) had been warned not to help the foreigners. Eventually they found a courageous man who would take them, even though he risked his life every step of the way. The women and children were crammed into a cart with a few possessions. James Liddell rode a mule. Under cover of darkness, they set off on their perilous journey.

Later in life Tom described his anguish as he sat alone in the bungalow. All that was dear to him in this world was in that cart, with death lurking at every turn. If they met the Boxers, there would be no mercy. The decision which he had reached a few hours before now seemed folly. Other missionary families stayed at their post, praying that the peril would pass, or they took their chances on the road together. To divide a family doubled the risk of disaster. He spent the night praying for his family, for the Liddells, for the driver and even for the pony. He prayed that Mrs Liddell would not miscarry and that the twins would not cry out. He prayed that the Boxers would be at drills or rain processions and that the cart would soon be beyond their reach.

Next morning Mister Heaven and Liu-i found him asleep in a chair. Their protests were strong and shrill. Why on earth had the *taifu* not gone with the others? His explanation about protecting the flock was brushed aside. Did he not understand that his presence provoked their enemies and put everyone in danger? They had no wish to donate their heads to the Boxers. Why die pointlessly?

Then Mister Heaven said something which touched Tom deeply. '*Taifu*, we were born in this place and we shall die in it, but you came thousands of miles to bring us the gospel. If anything befell you, it would cause us great distress.' That settled the matter.

Tom gathered up a few possessions and on the table he laid out his riding crop and two hats. One was a soft brown trilby he had bought in Glasgow. The other was a traditional Chinese cap, part of his dress as a physician. He had a horse in the compound and he was a competent rider. That was his way out. He spent the rest of the day sorting out and burning papers, expecting everything to be looted. From the town, Christians brought news of more atrocities and advice on the safest route. Tom described the scene:

> To my dying day I shall never forget the last hour of my stay in the town and district for which I had hoped and prayed such great things . . . Before leaving, those who were with me knelt down and we commended ourselves to the care of our common Father. It was most touching to listen to the prayers of those who were about to face torture and burning like so many in China in this awful time. The spirit they showed was magnificent and affected me deeply.

The Chinese did not usually show emotion before foreigners, but they wept as they embraced him. One man whom Tom thought weak in faith later met a martyr's death, singing a hymn as he was struck down:

> Mighty God, while angels bless Thee,
> May a mortal sing Thy praise.

About nine o'clock Tom slipped out of the compound. A part of the wall had been lowered to make way for an extension and the mob would easily swarm over it. In the dispensary bottles would be smashed, medicines destroyed and anything valuable looted before the place was set on fire. 'The darkest night of my life' was how Tom described it. In reality it was three nights before full moon and an enormous yellow orb hung over the tiled roofs. Without the moonlight, he could never have avoided the crowds who had been watching the Boxers at drill.

Suddenly a bullet whistled passed his head. He could not believe it – after all he had done to look like a Chinaman! He put his hand to his head and realized he had picked up the wrong hat. He crouched low in the saddle, spurred the horse on and left the uproar behind. He crossed the Daling River and headed for the hills. He rode for most of the night to put as much distance behind him as possible. The sky was clear and the hills were bathed in moonlight. Just before dawn he came to an ancestral burial ground dotted with pine trees. He dismounted and led the horse along the 'spirit paths' between the mounds. He tethered it, lay down and slept.

At dawn the sun rose like a huge red disc; it was going to be another scorching June day. Tom gathered his things and saddled the horse. It was tempting to linger in this quiet place but he must press on.

Suddenly a man emerged from behind a mound. Then another and another, until a score of them formed a circle around him. They had been camping in another part of the burial ground. Grasping swords and spears, they looked like figures in a Chinese opera. He saw the flash of scarlet scarves and knew they were Boxers. Was this how it would end, butchered in a graveyard, thousands of miles from home?

Then one of them stepped between him and the others. He said hoarsely, 'I know this man. No one touches him except over my dead body.' He turned to Tom. 'Go at once because I can't protect you. Ride!'

Tom scrambled into the saddle and galloped away, leaping over the mounds. Behind him he heard angry voices but no pursuit. Who was his saviour? He never discovered, but it must have been a grateful patient or the relative of one. God had protected his life once more. He rode throughout the day under the fierce sun, halting only briefly to rest. That night he dozed in the saddle and several times nearly slipped off. He reached the railhead the next day. There he found his family and the Liddells camped by the line. They had been unable to raise a rescue party and Grace had refused to go on. They were praying for a miracle, that Tom would follow and arrive safely.

The railway line was in the process of being built, but construction trains were running under armed guard and eventually the party reached the coast. The next entry in Tom's diary was written at Yingkou on the Liaodong peninsula, the seaport from which he and Grace had sailed three years earlier in a decrepit junk. Here they found a steamer which took them to Shanghai. The city was crowded with refugees and buzzed with stories of death and destruction.

*The Revd James and Mrs Mary Liddell. Baby Eric (later of* Chariots of Fire *fame) was born the year after they fled Chaoyang*
© Eric Liddell Centre

The Cochranes and Liddells had lost everything they possessed and in the London Missionary Society's compound, they received clothes, money and support. Mary Liddell's baby boy was born there on 27 August 1900. He was christened Robert and grew up to be a medical missionary in Hopei province. Their second son was Eric, the celebrated Scottish athlete and the hero of the 1981 film *Chariots of Fire*.

He was born in the following year in Tientsin and later went to school in England with the Cochrane boys.[2]

Tom's ordeal was not over. He developed a high fever, rigours and an agonizing headache. He had black water fever, a severe form of malaria in which the destruction of red blood cells turns the urine dark red. Even with modern treatment, it can kill up to a third of its victims. But God had brought Tom and his family to safety and had more work for him to do. The skill of the missionary doctors and nurses did the rest.

Thus Tom could count five occasions on which God had preserved his life. As soon as he was well enough, the Society sent him back to Scotland to recover. The family travelled via America and arrived back on 28 August 1900.

\*\*\*

While the Cochranes and Liddells were fleeing for their lives, the final act of the Boxer tragedy was being played out in Peking. Around 200,000 hungry rebels crowded into the city and outnumbered the Imperial Army. Some kind of order existed inside, but outside the city walls the Boxers and regular troops fought fiercely against a column of European troops who were trying to make their way up the railway line from Tientsin. The foreigners were repulsed and for a heady moment it seemed as if the Boxers would be the heroes of the Chinese Empire.

On 11 June the chancellor of the Japanese legation was killed and his body mutilated; the Chinese government narrowly averted a crisis. On 20 June a second outrage changed everything. Baron Clemens von Ketteler, the German minister, was ambushed in his sedan chair and shot dead.[3] Such a crime could not go unpunished and a full-scale invasion by the Great Powers was now inevitable. The next day Cixi threw in her lot with the Boxers and declared war on the alliance of Eight Nations.

---

[2] In 2015 the Chinese government recognized Eric's contribution to China's welfare and erected a statue to him in Tientsin.

[3] The reason has been much debated. Peking was awash with rumours, one of which alleged that Ketteler had shot and killed a Chinese boy suspected of being a Boxer spy. A more likely explanation was that he simply gave the boy a thrashing.

*Rebel Boxer soldiers in the Siege of the Legations*
An Underwood & Underwood stereophoto. Library of Congress, Prints & Photographs Division

A thousand Europeans and 400 troops took refuge in the legation quarter, which the Boxers promptly besieged. The civilians were
a mixture of diplomats, clerks, servants, merchants and missionaries with their families. The troops were a detachment of sailors and
marines of several nationalities who had arrived from Tientsin before
the railway line was closed; there were also 3,000 Chinese Christians,
mostly Roman Catholics. There were many acts of heroism and sacrifice by Europeans and Chinese. The Roman Catholic cathedral in
Peking and the European settlements at Tientsin were also besieged.

The relief column finally fought its way up to the city, broke the siege
and entered it on 14 August. The behaviour of some contingents was as
barbaric as that of the Boxers. Entire blocks were looted and destroyed
and anyone suspected of being a Boxer was summarily decapitated.
An Irish journalist, George Lynch, wrote, 'There are things that I must
not write, and that may not be printed in England, which would seem

to show that this western civilization of ours is merely a veneer over savagery.' Much of the savagery was displayed by the German soldiers, who arrived late and missed the fighting. It was in China (not in the trenches of the First World War) that they earned the reputation and nickname of Huns.[4] On the other hand the conduct of the Japanese troops was exemplary and they were regarded as showing great 'pluck'. That reputation would change with their invasion of China in 1937.

*Captured Boxer fighters awaiting execution. One man smokes unconcernedly*

An Underwood & Underwood stereophoto. Library of Congress, Prints & Photographs Division

---

[4] They owed the nickname to Kaiser Wilhelm II, who saw the German contingent off at Bremerhaven on 27 July. His farewell address included the words: 'Just as a thousand years ago, the Huns under their King Attila made a name for themselves . . . may the name German be affirmed by you in such a way in China that no Chinese will ever again dare to look cross-eyed at a German.' Wilhelm was famous for his public relations blunders.

It should be noted that at the height of the uprising more than half the imperial viceroys, provincial governors and mandarins refused Cixi's command to assist the Boxers and attack the foreigners. In many cases they went to great lengths to protect them. Without their courageous opposition, the outcome would have been much worse.

\*\*\*

The last part of this chapter makes painful reading. The Church in China paid a terrible price and Chinese Christians were the main target of the Boxers. Some were offered a mock tribunal and the chance to recant. Others were simply caught and hacked to death. Some were trussed up and laid on a village cutter, a machine with a weighted blade capable of chopping straw bales in two.

The Boxers took sadistic pleasure in torturing their victims. Tom wrote:

> Some were burned alive, some were burned at the stake, and some were anointed with kerosene and then set fire to. Some dashed their children's brains out to save the little ones from cruel torture. Some met their death singing and some met it saying, 'Father, forgive them for they know not what they do.'

Many families fled to the hills or hid in the wheat fields. To protect their older children, some parents were forced to smother their babies so that their crying would not give them all away.

In a typical atrocity, the newly planted church in Fanshi-hsien in Shanxi province was attacked and set on fire by a mob during a morning service on Sunday, 1 July 1900. The Chinese evangelist in charge was wounded and thrown into the flames, as were others who attempted to flee. Altogether 22 people, most of the congregation, were burned alive. It was estimated that throughout that province alone 8,000 Catholics died; the Protestant losses were far smaller.

The total number of Chinese Christians killed was never known because the Chinese government made no systematic enquiry, but from the missionaries' calculations it was probably more than 30,000, which was between 12 and 30 per cent of all Chinese believers at the time. Many pastors and their families were killed and entire churches were wiped out. Those who were allowed to live saw their homes looted and burned. They were left penniless and, with nobody to help them, they died miserably of cold and starvation that winter.

By no means did all the believers stand firm, for many were new in their faith and the pressure to recant was huge. But there were many heroes. They died refusing to bow down to an idol or to burn a pinch of incense. They died shielding missionary families and leading their children to safety. Many Protestants died when they might have survived. When confronted with the accusation 'You are of the T'ien Chu Kiao' (i.e. the Roman Catholic Church), they could have answered truthfully that they had nothing to do with the Catholics. Instead they said, 'We do not belong to the T'ien Chu Kiao *because we are of the Yeh-su Kiao.*' They refused to deny Jesus though it cost them their lives.

What of the foreign missionaries? Two hundred and thirty-nine were martyred, four-fifths of them Protestants and most of them British. They displayed the utmost courage, crying out to God to forgive their executioners. The China Inland Mission bore the heaviest loss, 79 souls. The missionaries whose lives were spared often suffered more than those who were killed immediately. If they could not reach the safety of the coast, they took to the hills and sheltered in caves for days or weeks on end. With no money or food and a price on their heads, their chances of survival were slim. They wrote farewell letters which they entrusted to friendly villagers.

Some of these letters found their way back to England and were published in a booklet titled *Martyred Missionaries of the China Inland Mission, with a Record of the Perils and Sufferings of Some Who Escaped.* Whenever I read it, I marvel at the courage and faith of these men and women, their concern for their Chinese converts, their love of their children and the pathos of their situation. They clung firmly to God's promises, while preparing themselves for a violent end and accepting that deliverance might lie that way. 'God does his very best and never makes mistakes,' wrote one man who was shortly to die. 'Death is but the gateway to heaven.'

In some cities all foreigners, not just the missionaries, were killed. Often they went to the *yamen* for protection, as Tom Cochrane and James Liddell nearly did, only to be executed as criminals. On 9 July in Taiyuan in Shanxi province, the anti-Western Governor Yu-Hsien (known as 'the Butcher of Shanxi') ordered the missionaries to attend his court, allegedly to take them into protective custody. A hostile mob gathered and the further details were unclear, but the outcome was that 45 Westerners were beheaded, together with many Chinese Christians. Their bodies were thrown to the dogs.

These events set a terrible precedent. It has been calculated that more men and women were martyred for their faith globally during the twentieth century than during the previous 2,000 years. And it all started in the spring of 1900 with the Boxers in northern China. A half-century later the Chinese Communists killed or starved to death an infinitely greater number of Christians.

But for believers persecution has to be seen in a biblical context. Jesus told his disciples to be prepared for it: 'Rejoice and be glad, because great is your reward in heaven, for in the same way they persecuted the prophets who were before you' (Matthew 5.12 NIV). The missionaries came to China knowing full well the dangers they faced when they left the safety of the treaty ports. They counted it a privilege to suffer in Jesus' name.

After the uprising was suppressed, all who survived returned to their former stations, apart from those who were broken in health. The Boxer Uprising discredited the use of violence towards foreigners and inaugurated what has been called 'the Golden Age' for mission in China (1901–25). By 1919 there were over 3,300 missionaries in the country, not counting their children; the figure reached a high-water mark of 8,000 in 1925. Within a short time rebuilding began and churches, chapels, schools and orphanages rose again, larger, better built and of more modern design. The gospel was preached with a new vigour and the number of believers rapidly increased. All this confirmed the saying of Tertullian, a first-century Christian writer: 'The blood of the martyrs is the seed of the Church.'

I cannot close this chapter without mentioning 28-year-old Flora Glover. She escaped with her husband and two small children from Lu-an in Shanxi province. For ten weeks they suffered unimaginable hardships of which her husband, the Revd Archibald Glover (1859– 1954), wrote a harrowing account titled *A Thousand Miles of Mira-*

*cles in China.* After her newborn daughter died, Flora wrote from her sickbed in Shanghai:

> My heart is daily praising God for the blessed experience He has given us as 'partakers in the sufferings of Christ' . . . We cannot yet say what the Mission will decide, and then my heart longs to return to Lu-an as soon as possible.

Flora never recovered her health and she died of dysentery on 25 October 1900, the last martyr of the uprising.

# 9

## *Back to Peking*

The next entry in Tom's diary, dated 1 September 1900, was written in his mother's house in Mount Pleasant Street in Greenock. It reads, 'Could anyone have told me that my next entry would be written in Scotland, I would have marvelled beyond measure. Yet such is the case.'

His health returned but he was tormented by the newspaper reports of those who had escaped the massacres.[1] He took long walks, remembering the faces of Christian brothers and sisters, both Chinese and British, praying that they were unharmed, interceding for the Church in Chaoyang, and pleading for the new converts and for his patients. He had no way of knowing what, if anything, was left of three years' work. A sense of guilt enveloped him like a mist on the River Clyde. His conscience accused him of not standing firm in the day of testing, a most awful thing. His diary spells it out: 'Should I not have said, instead of leaving Chaoyang when they wanted me to do so, "No! I shall stay with you and die with you"? . . . Oh my Father, hear my cries!'

It took all Grace's love and encouragement for Tom to accept what his relatives and everyone else saw clearly. His death would have achieved nothing; God had preserved him and his family for a purpose.

\*\*\*

At this point you may be excused for thinking that what the Cochranes needed next was some peace and quiet, a steady income and a good nursery school for the boys. That was what Tom's mother

---

[1] Some of these were reprinted from the *Shanghai Mercury*, an English-language newspaper, and circulated in missionary circles.

thought and it led to tearful family discussions. But there was no way that her son would budge. On the contrary, the Scottish air seemed to clear his head and sharpen his perspective. Overnight the vision of a medical school in Peking became keener, far more urgent. Now it was to be not just a centre for education but a riposte, a testimony in bricks and mortar that Christian love is infinitely greater than the powers of evil.

So it turns out that Tom owed several debts to the Boxer Uprising. Without it, he might have stayed in Mongolia eating his heart out until death or illness removed him. Without the physical devastation it caused, a unique need would not have arisen in Peking. And without the winds of political change which followed it, the conditions for a bold venture would not have arisen. As a Chinese proverb puts it, 'When the winds of change blow, some build walls and some build windmills.'

After a remarkably short time Tom wrote in his diary, 'I think I am now quite cured of any longing for home and shall be willing to return to China for life. Send me soon, Father.' Meanwhile he took up the customary work of missionaries on furlough: preaching, meeting supporters and raising funds. His day book contains the outline for a half-hour address with an appeal for more involvement by the Scottish churches. China's future hung in the balance. Would the nation continue in darkness or would it become a Christian country? Would the Protestant churches rise up or would Roman Catholicism resume its expansion? He challenged his hearers to pray and to get involved.

He also spent hours at Glasgow Medical School with professors and administrators, picking their brains. Learned men who a few years earlier thought that he had committed professional suicide saw him in a different light. Their former pupil, this son of Greenock, had turned out to be a hero; they were pleased to give advice about his remarkable plan for a medical school on the other side of the world. Tom's head was not turned. While others sang his praises, he shrugged them off, saying he had achieved little in three years: 'The Boxers chased me out and I hadn't much to show for it!'

\*\*\*

Meanwhile his future was being discussed over 400 miles away in London, where the London Missionary Society faced many problems. In their fury, the Boxers had destroyed scores of missionary hospitals which had done superb work over the years. For example they looted and burned the hospital in Hsiao Chang where Dr Sewell McFarlane had worked for 12 years.[2] McFarlane was appalled at the behaviour of local people who profited from the destruction,

> whose lives I have many and many a time saved from opium poisoning, and helped them through many an obstetric case and done endless kindnesses for them . . . to think that these should be the first to loot! My heart bleeds for our native Christians. Now we go, what will happen to them?

The answer was: *rebuild*. In Peking the Boxers destroyed all of the four missionary hospitals, including the Free Healing Hospital, the flagship of the London Missionary Society. It had been opened in 1861 by a legendary surgeon, William Lockhart (1811–96), one of the first Protestant medical missionaries to China, who once trod the boards at Guy's Hospital. He had arrived in 1838 and after many adventures moved to Peking in 1861 when it was opened up to foreigners. The British legation was pleased to have its own medical officer, but he met great hostility from the Chinese and worked under diplomatic protection.

Tom Cochrane had a great admiration for Lockhart, whose leatherbound journal was his treasured possession. In it Lockhart described his practice of approaching people on the streets of Peking who were suffering with eye complaints. In the dusty germ-laden air they were many and he could spot them at a few paces. He offered to treat them for free and was so successful that he was soon offered all manner of other diseases. His assistant registered as many as 500 patients in a day. Many were women, from one of whom he removed a large breast cyst in December 1861. It was the first operation to be performed by general anaesthetic in Peking.

Lockhart's practice extended from the poorest to the richest, or as he put it, 'I have every grade of button represented – red, blue, white and gold.' (He was referring to the button on a government official's hat

---

[2] Dr Sewell's predicament was mentioned on p. 74.

*The ruin converted to house the Free Healing Hospital of the
London Missionary Society, Peking*
Cochrane Family Collection

that denoted his rank.) He set up a hospital in a private house and then
succeeded in transferring it to a former Buddhist temple. Old photographs show a ramshackle building, but it was said to be the finest conversion in Asia. In the first two and a half years Lockhart treated 30,000
patients there. Over a period of 40 years it treated more than a million
patients, yet it rarely employed more than one European doctor.

In 1901 this building lay in ashes. The Home Board was looking
for someone to rebuild it and to coordinate the Society's medical
and evangelistic work in the capital. And who, somebody suggested,
was better qualified than the young Scottish doctor who had made a
vigorous start in Inner Mongolia and whom God had providentially
spared? He spoke and wrote Mandarin, he was a good organizer and
he was familiar with the Chinese way of thinking.

Senior missionaries also recalled that when they met Tom in Tientsin in 1897, they reported that he was 'a strong man' and had regretted

*The Free Healing Hospital of the London Missionary Society, Peking, March 1900, shortly before the Boxers destroyed it*
Cochrane Family Collection

that he was not posted to a large city with more scope for his abilities. Now that move was possible. After they discussed it, the board members were unanimous. Dr Thomas Cochrane was right for the job. He would be the Society's new man in Peking.

On 9 September 1901 Tom sailed for Shanghai on the *Kiautschou*, a 10,000-ton steamer with 65 passengers. Grace and the boys were not among them; the Society refused to send them on the grounds that Peking was too dangerous.

\*\*\*

And what of Chaoyang meanwhile? Conditions remained unsettled north of the Great Wall and, in James Liddell's words, mounted bandits were 'doing their own sweet will'. Nonetheless Liddell braved them to visit the town and his report answered the questions that caused Tom so much distress. Liddell found that Christians in Chaoyang had indeed been tortured and killed, the compound had been destroyed and much of the flock had scattered, but he was warmly welcomed by the remnant. He stayed for three months, helping to restore relationships between the believers and Boxer sympathizers who had persecuted them. Two native preachers and three elders accused of extorting compensation from their tormentors had to be suspended.

Eventually Liddell was able to write, 'We have seen quite a number of breaches healed and misunderstandings cleared up. Thus the work of reconstruction goes on. Time is a wonderful healer.' But there was no money to relaunch the station. The Liddell family was reassigned to Tientsin (where Eric was born in the same year) and the mission was handed over to Irish Presbyterians. They were already well established in north-east China, with nine stations.

***

During six weeks at sea Tom had plenty of time to think about a medical college, and the more he thought, the more daunting the idea became. There were too many unknowns. Would the Empress Dowager ever permit it to be built, let alone permit Chinese students to receive Christian instruction? Would the government approve foreign examinations and degrees? How many lecturers would he need and where would he find them? Would the other societies work with him? In a post-Boxer world, how could xenophobia be overcome?

He hoped for support from the expatriate community in Peking, but it was small and had far fewer hongs and influential taipans than Shanghai or Hong Kong. And few foreigners cared much for the welfare of those they called 'the natives'. They spoke an impossible language, ate revolting food and made obnoxious company. Life for most expatriates was taken up with an endless round of dinners, dances, bridge parties, tennis parties and race meetings. In the heat of summer they made for the resorts on the coast and continued the social round there.[3] The more thoughtful of them felt that the country was not

---

[3] Some were bored stiff. The wife of the Belgian ambassador wrote in 1907, 'Life is very dull in Peking in winter and some people would weep with boredom.' Certain diplomats never went outside the city, and the Spanish ambassador was reputed not to go outside the legation quarter.

ready for change; the abortive government reforms of 1898 seemed to have proved that. And surely a missionary's job was to relieve the natives' suffering and teach them religion, not medicine. Education should be left to the secular authorities.

There was a further source of prejudice. Both the Chinese and the foreigners who resorted to traditional physicians often concluded they were quacks who did nothing without demanding a fat fee in advance. Scientific training would simply make them more avaricious. Tom's reply was that he was making a fresh start with teachable young men. They would learn Christian ethics at the same time as they learned science.

Even if every other obstacle were miraculously overcome, the overwhelming problem remained: how on earth to finance and staff a medical college from scratch? Tom had no money and there was little enough of it in Peking. The few individuals who might help were already burdened and the government was bankrupted by the Boxer Indemnity. It was paying the equivalent of £67 million a year in silver (at the 1900 value) to the Great Powers. Thirty-nine years later this debt was still being paid off, at four per cent interest.

\*\*\*

With the teaching hospital, Tom was on firmer ground. He had been commissioned to rebuild the Free Healing Hospital which had enjoyed an excellent reputation and a sound financial base. The annual report for 1898 showed that 60 expatriates, including the British minister in Peking, contributed and that it was virtually self-supporting. No doubt altruism and self-interest went hand in hand. These people would surely welcome the return of the hospital and subscribe to the costs. The question was: could he turn it into a teaching hospital? That was a giant step, well beyond what the Home Board had expected. They had given him a mere £40 a year to start the work. It was barely half his salary.

The problems that lay before him required a range of skills far beyond those of the average missionary. But the years spent victualling ships on the Clyde had made him a canny negotiator, and those in Chaoyang had made him a manager, a builder and a linguist. What he lacked in skills others would provide, but as the ancient Chinese proverb says, 'A journey of one thousand miles starts with a single step.' Only Tom could take the step of faith that would persuade others. He spent two weeks at the London Missionary Society's headquarters in Shanghai, where he doubtless had some interesting talks with senior men on the spot. Then he took the steamer to Tientsin and arrived in Peking on 31 October 1901.

*Peking before the Boxer Uprising, from a city wall*
John Thomson. Wellcome Collection

Peking was already ancient when Kublai Kahn made it his capital in 1267. In those days it was called Cambaluc; in 1901 the Mongols still called it the city of the Great Khan. Its streets and gates were as he had ordered them, but over the centuries the place had grown. It was three cities in one; it had walls within walls and gates within gates. The streets ran from north to south and from east to west with mathematical precision. The main avenues were so broad that 20 riders on horseback could gallop abreast along them. In the old days the massive gatehouses had housed 10,000 men to protect the city. Now the authorities locked the gates at night and latecomers either bribed the gatekeepers or found lodgings outside.

*Peking after the siege of 1900. Extensive damage was done by both the Boxers and rampaging foreign troops*

The American missionary Isaac Headland described Peking in 1894:

It is the greatest and best preserved walled city in the empire, if not in the world. The Tartar City is sixteen miles in circumference, surrounded by a wall sixty feet thick at the bottom, fifty feet thick at the top and forty feet high, with six feet of balustrade on the outside, beautifully crenellated and loop holed, and in a good state of preservation. In the centre of the Tartar City is the Imperial City, eight miles in circumference, encircled by a wall six feet thick and fifteen feet high, pierced by four gates at the points of the compass, and in the centre of this again is the Forbidden City, occupying less than half a square mile, the home of the court.

In 1901 the city of nearly 750,000 inhabitants was in bad shape. It lay like an old dragon licking its wounds after a savage beating. During the Siege of the Legations, the Boxers had destroyed the commercial quarter, the richest part of the city. They stripped the stores and warehouses of their silks and furs, and burned them down. Most of the buildings were wooden and burned easily. They emptied the jewel shops of anything the owners did not bury. They looted palaces, private homes and public buildings before setting them on fire. The Chien Men, a superbly carved mediaeval city gate with a tower a hundred feet high, was an icon of imperial power. When it went up in flames, the terrified inhabitants thought the end of the world had come. The library of the Hanlin Academy, a cultural treasure dating from the eighth century, was also burned down and thousands of irreplaceable volumes were lost.

When the foreign troops relieved the siege, a second orgy of destruction occurred. Contemporary photographs show parts of Peking looking like Germany's industrial cities in 1945, reduced to rubble by aerial bombardment. Tom saw yellowing notices in English placed by shop owners which begged the 'Sirs' to do them no harm. One read pathetically, 'We are all good men here.' Another said, 'No looting – nothing left.'

On the other hand the permanent presence of foreign troops (which was permitted for the first time by the treaty) brought benefits too. The main streets were tarmacked and electric lamps installed. New restaurants and teahouses sprang up and livery stables from which one could hire pony carts and smart broughams drawn by trotting Mongol ponies. There were even a few motor cars. There was a hotel which would later become the celebrated Grand Hôtel de Pékin, but in 1901 it was little more than a boarding-house.

Much of the city was not damaged and of it Tom could write, 'It's a far cry from Mongolia!' Palaces and mansions stood in grounds dotted with lily ponds and fountains and guarded by high walls. In the streets, nobles in silks and furs rode in painted Peking carts, accompanied by a mounted escort. Concubines with almond eyes and tiny painted mouths were whisked along in sedan chairs. Foreign cavalry rode haughtily through the streets, giving way to no one. Flashy prostitutes with slit skirts tripped in and out of the Houses of Joy.

Alongside these scenes of prosperity and grandeur there was a squalor more vile than that of Chaoyang. Much of the city comprised slums of one-storey buildings with roofs of blackened tiles, traversed by alleys seething with filth. Courtyards were covered with heaps of rubbish and excrement which no one thought to remove. Dogs scavenged everywhere and the roofs of the palaces were laden with crows. The stench was unbearable and in addition the city (even in 1901) was blighted by a smog created by countless coal-burning stoves. Every day a column of two-humped Bactrian camels swayed up the streets, disdain etched on their grimy muzzles. They carried a pannier of coal on either flank, 400 pounds of coal per beast.

The difference between Chaoyang and Peking, Tom concluded, was that in the former everyone was poor and struggling to survive; here the wealthy rode by dead bodies in the gutters without turning their heads.

\*\*\*

*Dr Li Hsiao Ch'uan, who worked for 30 years at the Free Healing Hospital and was Tom Cochrane's friend and ally*
Cochrane Family Collection

In the compound of the London Missionary Society, Tom was greeted by a man called Li Hsiao Ch'uan who had been chief assistant to Eliot Curwen, the last doctor at the old hospital. He had 30 years of experience in Western medicine and was referred to as Dr Li. He proved a good friend and ally to Tom in the years ahead. Dr Li had experienced several miraculous escapes from the Boxers. He was sheltered by influential patients. They tried to make him adopt devices for his own safety, like keeping idols and shoes made of silver paper on display in his rooms. The latter were burned as a graveside offering to the spirits, so people would naturally conclude that Dr Li was not a Christian. He resolutely declined to play these tricks and he survived unharmed.

When Tom was shown the site of the ruined hospital, he noted down Li's words: '"In forty years we have treated a million patients – and now we are reduced to this!" As he spoke he pointed to a heap of broken bricks and two partly burned poles which had stood for two centuries.' The poles were nearly 70 feet tall. They were flagstaffs that had marked the entrance of the Buddhist temple that had been on that site. The Boxers tried to burn them but they did not succeed, and the locals took that for a good omen. Later Tom had them restored and smartly lacquered.

From the top of the rubble Tom saw in the distance the yellow roofs of temples and palaces in the Forbidden City, looking like gigantic upturned boats rising among the trees. Somewhere beyond the gatehouses and 'dragon bridges' was the Throne Room, where the Emperor sat at the centre of the world, wielding immense authority over millions of subjects. Tom wrote later, 'Under a sudden impulse, I prayed that God would somehow enable me to touch one of the oldest thrones in the world.'

It was a bold request. The throne was effectively occupied by the Empress Dowager whose political rule already spanned four decades. She was said to hate missionaries and to have told a diplomat's wife:

> They inoculate our people with the virus of Christianity and the
> Christian Chinese immediately lose all respect for our laws and
> customs. Most of the trouble in inland China is caused by Christian
> Chinese. They refuse to honour their rulers and the lesser officials set
> over them by these rulers.

Because of her conduct during the uprising she had the blood of thousands of Christians on her hands. Could this proud and bigoted old woman ever be persuaded to change?

\*\*\*

It was not Tom's way to stand around waiting for things to happen. From the rubble he spotted a disused grain shop next to some stables. On the face of it they were not much of a prize but he went to see the owner all the same. When the man heard of the plan for a dispensary he offered the buildings for free. (Later Tom bought them.) That was a good start because for the moment Tom had to fund everything out of his £40 a year. 'I have to find money for drugs, instruments, dressings, coal, repairs and general hospital utensils etc.'

The grain shop proved as dirty and dilapidated as the dispensary in Chaoyang, and unsurprisingly it also had rats scampering in the ceiling. Tom's new ally Dr Li tracked down orderlies who had worked at the old hospital and were glad to work again. They swept, scrubbed and whitewashed. The stables, which had housed mules, underwent an Augean cleansing and became wards, albeit few and small.

Soon Tom moved in. He hung a signboard outside, and in no time beggars, peddlers and outcasts were queuing up, bringing with them all the parasites and pestilences of China. For them the stables were paradise, for they had nothing. His first question to them was '*Chi fan me la?*' ('Have you eaten yet?'), which is a common form of greeting. Of course the answer was always no. He struggled to provide food out of a slender purse.

\*\*\*

It is impossible for doctors like me who have only practised medicine in an affluent Western society to imagine the lives of people who belonged to what Tom called 'the beggar class'. They were so numerous in Chinese cities that they were divided into guilds which shared out the begging spots. In summer, they drowsed in the sun and rose like wraiths at the approach of a stranger, piteously rattling their bowls, displaying their withered arms, sores, goitres, rickety legs and self-inflicted wounds. In winter they put on all the rags they possessed and shivered in their hovels. Any coins they begged went on opium that left them senseless. They lived a life of helpless bad luck. The simplest accident or infection could be fatal.

*China's cities teemed with beggars like this man, who called himself
the King of the Beggars. They organized themselves into guilds and
controlled the best begging spots*

An Underwood & Underwood stereophoto. Library of Congress, Prints & Photographs Division

Some had once been part of the city's porterage force, a barefoot
army whose members moved everything from bricks and food to
sedan chairs and rickshaws. They were known as 'coolies', and would
often use a six-foot bamboo pole to balance a load which would crip-
ple a European.[4] Contemporary photographs show them mingling
with the crowds or standing on street corners, looking out for work.

---

[4] Today the word 'coolie' is considered offensive. In Tom Cochrane's day it simply meant
a labourer who worked hard for very little pay. Coolies were often indentured and little better than slaves. Only later did the word become a term of racist abuse.

They laboured for a few *cash* a day until they were broken by arthritis or opium and took to begging.

Beggars had no proper names, only nicknames like 'Old Yi' or 'Lame Leg Wong'. The city authorities provided an Imperial House of Refuge with heated *kangs*, but the conditions were so loathsome and deaths so common that most beggars preferred to doss wherever they could. There were entire families and tribes of beggars. Tom described a family of seven living on the equivalent of four pence a day, and a grandmother starving by degrees, eating only one day in three, yearning to die so that her family would have more. Another elderly patient living on her own existed on a handful of roasted chaff a day.

When a beggar knew that his (or her) end was near, he did not even raise his eyes at a coin dropped in his cup. Then one day his spot on the street was empty, his body was thrown on the refuse cart and his rags were divided up. There was nobody to care for his grave so he had no hope of an afterlife. Even in death there was no comfort. In Canton the authorities set aside a special place for the poor to go and die. Logically enough it was called the Dying Field.

The most pathetic beggars were the children whose parents or owners blinded or mutilated them to add to their appeal. Some survived by working punch machines and spinning wheels in the sweatshops, chained to them for 12 hours a day. Other waifs were dressed in bright colours and hired out in pairs to depraved clients. The situation was no different from other Asiatic cities where countless children were enslaved. As late as the 1920s the British authorities in Hong Kong struggled to eradicate slavery.

All the patients in the stables were of 'the old hundred names', an affectionate term for the common people. Whole families squatted in the stables, spreading their bedrolls on the floor and setting up kettles and cooking pots. The result was chaotic and the chance of catching typhus from flea-ridden bedclothes increased with numbers. But the relatives performed two important functions: they fed their loved ones and they provided nursing care. Trained nurses were rarer in China than doctors. The well-off were looked after by their servants and the poor by their family members, if they had any.

Dying patients were frequently dumped on the doorstep and left to expire. In winter, when night temperatures in Peking plummet to minus 20 degrees Celsius, beggars in their hovels developed frostbite which turned to gangrene. At such times Tom's amputation kit was in frequent use. He was also kept busy fitting patients with wooden limbs. Things had changed little in the capital; 40 years earlier William Lockhart reported treating beggars whose gangrenous feet dropped off, leaving the bones protruding. One man lost half a leg when he lay insensible across a charcoal fire.

Tom's facilities were plain and simple. His examination room was a former kitchen ten feet by eight; the operating room the same size, with a floor of broken bricks and soft light coming through the paper windows. The equipment was rudimentary. For example, when he needed an incubator for bacteriological cultures, he placed a biscuit tin over a spirit lamp and pushed a thermometer through the lid. The operating table was a slab of wood set on trestles. Nonetheless Tom could write, 'Soon after my arrival I was doing all kinds of major operations with marvellously good results.'

\*\*\*

The beggars were not the only victims of this merciless society. There was a high suicide rate from despair, particularly the despair of opium addiction. Every conceivable method was employed and every poison tried: opium chiefly, then mercury, lead (often in the form of white face powder), oil and even phosphorus. One young woman waited until her family was asleep before swallowing the heads of several boxfuls of matches, followed by all the kerosene she could find.

One of Tom's attempted suicide cases turned into a black comedy. The patient cut his throat with a razor, but it had a short stubby blade and was no good for the purpose. He botched the job, making a hole in his windpipe and losing a lot of blood but leaving the great vessels intact. Furious at his failure, he plunged headfirst down a well. The water at the bottom covered his nose and mouth but did not reach his neck. He was stuck upside down, breathing through the newly made hole.

His friends yanked him out by the heels and asked the foreign doctor to stitch him up. It was late and Tom was exhausted after a long day, but he set about inserting the sutures, while the fellow glared furiously at him. Tom realized that, back in Chaoyang, Liu-i could have done the job perfectly well. He wondered, 'How much longer must I do things that I can teach to others?'

The wealth of suffering around him nearly broke Tom's heart but it also strengthened his resolve. Time and again it reminded him why he was there. He was not called to take up the traditional role of the missionary among the poor, although he would do what he could. No, a medical college and a teaching hospital – they were his goal.

\*\*\*

Tom's work did not go unnoticed in the city. Educated Chinese heard about it and were amazed that a foreigner would take such pains over beggars, pedlars and opium addicts. There was some softening of attitudes, but he did not find life in Peking easy. The constant hubbub of the streets, the smells and the crowds troubled him. Foreigners were no longer a rarity, but he was often followed by fellows who mocked him with grunting noises. Men on the hot-pot stands and tofu vendors held out food and shouted, '*Chi, chi, chi*', a jeering invitation to buy and eat. He longed for happier days when he wore a pigtail and Chinese clothes and blended into the background.

He also missed his family. Two days after arriving in the capital, he complained to the Home Board in London: 'At Singapore I got my first letter of welcome from Peking accompanied by the enquiry "Why are you not bringing your wife from England? There is no reason whatever why she should not come."'

He asked for his family to be sent out as soon as possible. 'Address your wire "Cochrane, Peking" and simply give the steamer's name.' Then followed a Scotsman's postscript: 'Please also pay my wife the usual outfit money. It will be five years since she had any and the children have never had any at all.'

In February 1902 he described the house he had rented. It was basic and he teased the Home Board members with an ironic comment: 'If you want to make some people content with their lot, send them to a place like Chaoyang for a few years and you will have no trouble!'

*An elegant Peking cart painted on silk. The moustachioed face just
visible at the window is thought to represent Thomas Cochrane*
Author's collection

Soon after the arrival of Grace and the boys, a dramatic accident
reminded Tom of his prayer about touching the throne. He was walking through the Imperial City when he heard a wild clatter of hooves.
A runaway pony cart bore down on him, the driver straining desperately at the reins as he tried to head it off. At the last moment the
pony swerved and the occupant, a middle-aged man dressed in silks
and furs, was thrown out. Thud! He landed with considerable force at
Tom's feet.

Tom gaped. The cart was painted in the yellow colours of the Imperial Court. The passenger struggled to maintain his dignity as Tom
helped him to his feet and brushed him down. His cap had fallen on a
dunghill. It bore a ruby button, the mark of an imperial prince. Tom
retrieved it with a bow and introduced himself. 'Sir, I am Dr Cochrane
of the London Missionary Society. Are you hurt? Are you in pain? Is
there anything I can do for you?' A small crowd had gathered and were
staring at the barbarian who dared to address a nobleman on the street.

The latter noted the European clothes, the flawless Mandarin and
the respectful air. He shook his head and climbed shakily back into

the cart, with a bow in Tom's direction. When the cart had gone, Tom turned to a bystander and asked who he had been addressing. The man grinned. Did he not know? It was the Venerable Buddha's favourite minister, Prince Su.

*Prince Su, a Manchu prince married to a Mongolian princess. He was one of the Empress Dowager's favourite ministers*

An Underwood & Underwood stereophoto. Library of Congress, Prints & Photographs Division

Shanqi, the tenth Prince Su of the First Rank (1866–1922), was a Mongolian prince married to a Manchu princess and one of the most powerful men in the land. He had estates south of Peking, a fine *fu* (palace) in the legation quarter and a suite of rooms in the Forbidden City. His Su Wang Fu palace sheltered 300 Chinese converts during the Siege of the Legations, though whether he volunteered the protection or was forced to do so by American troops is unclear.

Tom could scarcely contain his excitement when he told Grace the story and described how the pony dumped the prince at his feet. What a canny beast that was! And could it be only chance that made it happen? Wasn't it a step closer to the throne? Grace could only think that God moved in mysterious ways. If it was the Lord's doing, more of the same might happen. Meanwhile, Tom should wait and see.

He decided to express his faith in God's grace by walking three times around the Imperial City. If Mongolians could crawl for miles on their bellies to grovel at their shrines, surely he could manage a brisk walk. It proved rather more demanding, for he had not realized that the Imperial City was eight miles in circumference. As he walked he prayed for the Emperor and the Empress Dowager, the court, the princes and the government officials. He prayed for the teeming millions of China and its beggars. He prayed for his fellow missionaries. And he prayed for money.

The prayer about money was answered in an unexpected way. The Great Powers took a hard line on damage done by the Boxers to European property and, as I have described, they exacted huge reparations. James Hudson Taylor refused to accept compensation on behalf of the China Inland Mission and gave it away to help found Shanxi University. He did this, he explained, 'in order to demonstrate the meekness and gentleness of Christ to the Chinese'. It was an act which amazed many.

Other missionaries reacted differently. They were determined to get justice for colleagues and converts who had lost everything they owned. A Congregational minister called William Ament, a hero of the Siege of the Legations, led something of a punitive expedition to recover goods, with an escort of the US Sixth Cavalry. He was heavily (and probably unfairly) criticized by the anti-imperialist Mark Twain for looting and extortion. Others joined in the slanging match, which went on for some years.

The London Missionary Society also received compensation and dedicated part of it to rebuilding the Free Healing Hospital. Much to his delight, Tom now had a budget of 7,000 taels of silver. But it was intended for the hospital, not the medical school, and it was a fraction of what he needed.

# 10

## *The Blue Death*

A faded photograph of the stables and grain shop shows Tom standing outside tumbledown buildings with five Chinese orderlies. Although he described these facilities in the East City as wretched and inadequate, they did good service and 1902 was a busy year. He saw 17,199 patients and treated 185 on his wards, 'if I may designate the rooms with that term'. He opened three more dispensaries outside Peking which acted as feeders to the main dispensary as well as what he cheekily called 'a hospital in the country', probably a dispensary with a few extra beds attached. He needed somewhere to discharge surgical patients for convalescence when he dared not send them back to their squalid homes.

Tom dreamed of bringing health care and preventative medicine into the community. His diary records what he spent on all these buildings and how he tried to persuade local people to subscribe to the costs. But money was so scarce that he was forced to introduce charges for those able to pay, while continuing to treat the beggars free as he had done in Chaoyang. It was a difficult decision, especially because the government was proposing to build its own hospitals, which would be free. But the reason was clear. 'The poverty we see is heartbreaking, but by charging those who can pay, we are all the better able to help those who cannot.'

\*\*\*

The house which the Cochranes rented had one low storey, like nearly all homes in Peking at that time. It was off a *hutong*, an alley that was part of a network of alleys. They lived at close quarters with other families around a complex of courtyards. When a neighbour beat his wife, she screamed back at him and everyone shared in the drama.

In summer the city stank like a cesspit, so when friends offered the Cochranes the use of a bungalow in the Western Hills, they accepted gratefully. The hills encircle the capital to the west and north, and from them the Great Wall starts its journey of 10,000 miles and more. Many Europeans had built holiday bungalows in these beautiful surroundings and Grace took the boys there for the summer while Tom stayed in the city. He visited them occasionally for two or three days. Later in life Robert remembered the pattern. 'Father was a workaholic and remained at work when all other Europeans were on vacation.'

The bungalow proved a blessing in view of what happened next. Peking was caught up in a cholera disaster. A world pandemic started in India in 1899 and claimed the lives of 800,000 there and 20,000 in the Philippines before reaching China. Of all the diseases of the ancient world, cholera was the most feared. It came on at lightning speed; a man might eat a good breakfast and feel fine, but if it had contained one drop of infected water, he could be dead by teatime. Life ebbed away in explosions of thin watery diarrhoea, up to 20 litres a day. They called it the Blue Death, because the skin sometimes turns blue-grey from dehydration.

In 1902 Peking's population lay helpless before the threat. Its water came from wells alongside the main streets and from springs in the Summer Palace which were connected to the city by an open canal. The opportunities for infection were limitless. As a rule the Chinese did not use cold water for drinking or washing – they thought that the latter would rob them of resistance to the cold – and they had no idea of how to make it safe. The Imperial Government knew nothing of bacteria, and public health laws were unheard of. 'One feels so helpless in the presence of the awful dirt and ignorance that abounds,' Tom wrote despairingly.

In May rumours began to circulate that cholera was in Peking and spreading. Tom lost one patient and knew of other deaths, but he had no idea what was happening across the city. How could he know? The government collected no statistics.

LE CHOLÉRA

*The Grim Reaper bringing death by cholera to Turkish troops*
*(illustration in* Le Petit Journal, *December 1912)*

Soon after Grace and the boys left for the country, the queues at his dispensary dwindled and the wards emptied, just as they had in Chaoyang when the Boxers came. People described death carts scooping up corpses like garbage. Burial rituals were abandoned in the haste to get them out of the city. In China no burials were permitted within a city's limits. One patient told Tom that he had stood at a city gate for four hours and counted 80 coffins leaving. And that was only at one gate. Children were dying in every street and people were desperate. It was the worst disaster they had ever known. For the sake of the children, could the good doctor not do something to help?

It was an astonishing request, for Tom had never heard a Chinese plead with a Westerner for his people. And yes, the good doctor could do something. The principles of controlling cholera had been known in England since 1854, when Dr John Snow removed the handle from a contaminated water pump in Soho. Students at Glasgow Medical School got a thorough training in applied epidemiology.

But there was a problem. Tom had no position and no authority. In Peking the hierarchy in the British community was as rigid as among the Chinese. At the top was the British minister with his legation and consular staff. Next came the bankers, the advisers and a drove of businessmen and engineers, then the travel writers, teachers and other Sinologues. A bunch of fugitives and soldiers of fortune came last. The missionaries probably came somewhere between the Sinologues and the fugitives. They were an embarrassment even to churchgoers. They ate Chinese food and went about in wheelbarrows. The clever ones spoke Mandarin and a few even wore Chinese clothes and a pigtail.

But the epidemic was growing and Tom was desperate. He decided to appeal to Sir Robert Hart, head of the Imperial Maritime Customs Service since 1863. As we saw in an earlier chapter, Hart occupied a unique position in government circles; though a British administrator, he was a zealot for China's best interests. He was also widely respected for his powers of diplomacy and had helped to negotiate the Boxer Protocol the previous year. Tom did not know him personally but was convinced that he could help.

When they met, Hart was impressed by the young Scot's passionate appeal. This concern for the Chinese was very different from the lofty attitude of those with whom he usually dealt. He came straight to the point. Dr Cochrane was the medical expert; what did he suggest?

Tom explained that the government officials were paralysed and people had no way of protecting themselves because no one knew what to do. The death rate could be halved immediately by simple measures; otherwise the epidemic would continue to spread. If he drafted a list of public health orders, could Sir Robert get them posted around the city?

Sir Robert thought for a moment. No, he had no authority for that, but he knew a man who had, an enlightened nobleman. He would give Tom an introduction. He dashed off a note and sealed it with a wax stamp.

When Tom read the envelope, he drew a breath. Hart asked if the doctor had met Prince Su? In a manner of speaking, Tom replied, but they had not been properly introduced. Hart was sure the prince would cooperate and Tom was left with the same feeling he had when Su landed at his feet. A higher power was directing the course of events.

Hart's note opened doors which had never before opened to a missionary. In no time Tom found himself in Prince Su's apartment in the Forbidden City. The prince was reclining in a throne-like chair, wearing a jacket embroidered with pearls and a cap with a ruby button which looked familiar. He welcomed Tom courteously and read the note. There was no hint of coolness, and if he remembered tumbling out of the cart at Tom's feet, etiquette prevented both of them from mentioning it. He thanked Tom for coming and invited him to draw up his recommendations immediately. His servants would see that they were posted throughout the city that day.

Tom wrote out a list of public health measures that would have done credit to Glasgow Medical School. They explained the role of bacteria and how to reduce the risk of infection. They directed the people to refrain absolutely from unboiled water and from eating ice, raw vegetables and fruit. They must eat only well-cooked food. Anything contaminated by vomit or faeces had to be burned, especially the straw on which the victims were nursed. Quarantine must be imposed. Instructions were also given on how to disinfect rooms by burning sulphur and scattering lime.

These instructions, which Tom sketched out in his day book, have a historical significance. They represent the first public health campaign on modern lines in China.

When the posters went up around the city, children ran to get their parents. Those who could not read begged others to tell them what to do. The number of new cases and of deaths fell immediately and the disease did not spread beyond the city, but thousands more died before the epidemic ended.

\*\*\*

The cholera epidemic was a turning point in Tom's fortunes; overnight he had shot up the social ladder and now he was a man in demand. Through the friendship of Sir Robert Hart, he was appointed medical adviser to the Chinese government and to the Imperial Chinese Maritime Customs. He served as consultant to the British and several other legations, which helped his budget considerably.

He had also made a friend in Prince Su, a man of charm, intelligence and hospitality. Tom was driven regularly in an imperial cart to the prince's apartments in the Forbidden City. In those sumptuous surroundings he found wealth and privilege that he had never seen before. The Manchus had enjoyed power, land and servants for generations. Their dress and their cuisine were highly sophisticated. Tom ate with ivory chopsticks off silver dishes that were laden with suckling pig, mandarin fish, plovers' eggs, truffles and spiced soups. Sometimes there were as many as 20 or 30 courses and it was impossble to refuse the morsels which the Prince himself proffered. To demur was a politeness which nobody took seriously. So please eat on, *taifu*, as noisily as you wish, with much smacking of lips and thunderous eructation to show your enjoyment in the Chinese way.

What a contrast with life in the mule stables! There he was surrounded by members of 'the old hundred families'. When he shared a simple midday meal with them, he gave thanks to God, and a score of grubby hands dipped eagerly into the same pot of rice. The fare was simple and there was not much of it, but the atmosphere was goodness and compassion. The name and love of Jesus were constantly on the lips of Tom's staff. The patients were bowled over by this warmth and were open to the gospel message. In Prince Su's apartment Tom was welcomed with every courtesy and kindness, but the minds of the nobles were hard and closed.

Somehow the man from Greenock found the grace of God in both situations. His ability to adapt to them is reminiscent of Rudyard Kipling's poem, written a few years later:

> If you can talk with crowds and keep your virtue,
> Or walk with kings nor lose the common touch . . .

Tom walked with princes and princesses and never lost the common touch.

His friendship with Prince Su also opened up professional opportunities at court. Suspicion melted as Su's family and friends confided in Tom about illnesses that had defeated their own doctors. Their custom when faced with a chronic ailment was to call in one doctor after another until, through skill or chance, the patient improved. The last doctor to call was credited with the cure.

Tom was not the first Western physician to be consulted at court; a Canadian female physician had treated ladies in the Empress Dowager's family, and a legation doctor was once called to the Emperor in an emergency. But he was the first male doctor to attend patients regularly in the Forbidden City. High government officials invited him to their homes, which was a significant breakthrough. A generation earlier any social contact had been impossible. Now Tom was able to give his hosts an object lesson in Christian love and care. Even traditional Chinese doctors sought his help. One wept for a patient he could not cure: 'He is my son, my only son!' Tom wrote of this man, 'The human touch of his appeal and my response made us friends.'

\*\*\*

A doctor's visit to a well-off family was a ceremonial affair for which he arrived by sedan chair or cart. There were rules to be observed: a great deal of bowing, a tea ceremony, polite questions and oblique answers. At the right moment, a suggestion was made in an offhand way. Since the good doctor was here, would he care to see an elderly relative who happened to be ailing a little?

It was not all plain sailing. Some of these families had suffered many indignities during the foreign occupation. One man remarked to Tom in an unguarded moment, 'What pleasure it would be to make my bed on the skin of a foreigner!'

In one strange incident a government official asked Tom to see his *tai tai* or number one wife. He was ushered in with the usual formalities. The lady was dressed in Manchu style in a long gown, platform shoes and a fan-shaped headdress, containing enough pins to secure a tent in a gale. He asked for her hand to take her pulse. This was the stock way of commencing a physical examination. Instead she took Tom's hand in hers. *Thptt!* A gobbet of spit landed on his palm. He blinked. What was she thinking of? Behind the flawlessly layered make-up he saw no emotion. Had he failed to observe some etiquette? Was it a deliberate insult? He never found out. He wrote in his diary, 'It was then that I realised more clearly my audacity in hoping to influence the Empress on the Throne. If anyone had heard me praying that, they would have thought me mad!'

These high-ranking Manchus and Chinese were proud and taught never to display their emotions. They were pragmatists; romantic poems were not a part of their culture and their marriages seemed loveless. The men had several wives and kept concubines; only the poor Chinese knew the challenges and the joys of monogamy. Marriages were arranged by go-betweens using horoscopes and divination and sealed by financial compacts. There was no regard for a girl's feelings in the matter; indeed she was not permitted to have any. From early childhood, girls and boys were kept apart and friendship would have been indecent.

So much, then, for romance in high places; the stereotype of the 'calm inscrutable Oriental' rang true. One man asked Tom to see a wife who was seriously ill. 'She's my fifth and she has a foul temper. Don't try too hard to cure her – I'm only asking for the sake of appearances.' Later he called Tom back and added, 'On second thoughts, you can try a little. My family burial ground is full, and if she dies before me I'll have to buy a new plot.'

\*\*\*

The practice of binding women's feet presented missionaries in China with another dilemma. It was a thousand years old and caused millions of women to suffer horribly, yet the population was hugely attached to it. In Chaoyang Tom had barely been aware of foot-binding. The Manchurians as the ruling class were exempt, the Mongolians would not countenance it and the Chinese peasant women needed to work in the fields; they slapped around happily in cloth shoes with feet as flat as a flounder. In Peking, however, binding was the rule in any family that claimed to be respectable, regardless of its income. It was a matter of conformity and face.

At some time between the ages of four and nine, a girl's feet were soaked in a mixture of herbs and animal excreta to soften the tissues. Their joints were deliberately dislocated and their toes forced downwards like the flap on an envelope until the nails pressed into the sole. (For that reason the practice might equally have been called *foot-breaking*.) Toes and sole were then drawn together by a swathe of bandages which were tightened every day until the foot was an inverted U around a hoof-like cleft. The dislocation of joints was usually done in midwinter because it was thought to hurt less when the feet were cold.

The aim was a 'Golden Lotus Foot' that was allegedly three and a half inches long and would not grow again even if unbound. In fact it was a *trompe d'oeil*: the folded toes were crammed into a tiny triangular shoe which was all that was visible, peeping beneath the woman's full-length gown. The heel and most of the sole were unaffected so that the overall length remained six to seven inches. The result was functionally ruinous. Binding left the child unable to walk properly, let alone to run or jump. She was forced to hobble in small steps with her knees slightly bent. She could not squat (an important position in Chinese culture) nor rise without difficulty. Arthritis of the hips was common in later life.

Much has been written about the reasons for this mutilation. One fanciful explanation is that centuries earlier a beautiful princess was born with club feet and that she concealed them by having them bound. Her beauty and ingenuity were such that others imitated her. The truth was that binding was an aspect of male domination. Throughout her life a woman was subject to the will of a man – to her father during her childhood, to her husband during her marriage and to her son in her widowhood. Chinese men cynically believed that foot-binding kept a woman out of mischief because she could not leave the house to gad about. Her place was in the home and she had no reason to leave it. For some reason men also found tiny feet erotic and the women's gait dainty; they compared the latter to 'lilies bowing in the wind'. Apparently the idea of female helplessness aroused the beast in them. Europeans on the other hand thought that Chinese women walked like hobbled mules.

The women rarely complained; the custom was so deeply embedded that it had become self-justifying. A girl with tiny feet was attractive, but a girl with 'large' feet was ugly and had no chance in the marriage market. She must have Lotus Feet to make a good match. If binding was delayed, many children begged for it to save them from ridicule.

The dilemma for missionaries was that they were taught not to interfere in cultural traditions unless they were clearly considered a sin. Foot-binding was a borderline case; some preached against it, while others stayed silent. Medical missionaries who saw the medical complications first-hand tended to speak out. It was frustrating to be called to a case of gangrene and to try to save the toes, knowing that as soon as the treatment was complete, the binding would be replaced.

The wives of missionaries were also outspoken, and in 1874 a group of Christian women in Amoy formed the first Western anti-foot-binding society. In Peking Mary Porter, the wife of an American missionary, and her friends did their best to find Christian husbands for young women with unbound feet. But they only succeeded among the educated. In 1895 Alicia Little (née Bewicke), a secular reformist and feminist, founded Tian Zu Hui, the Natural Foot Society. It drew together abolitionists of all kinds from the Chinese and foreign communities.

The Empress Dowager finally banned foot-binding to appease the foreigners after the Boxer Uprising but the order was rescinded. In 1912 the Republic of China again outlawed the practice, but ignorance and pride kept it going in remote areas. It continued as late as the 1940s.

Binding did not trouble the paupers in Tom's stables. Nor were they emotionally inhibited like the privileged classes. When they saw that Tom listened sympathetically, they shed floods of tears as they described their suffering and that of their friends. And they were so good to each other! One man who could only afford one small meal a day seemed slow in recovering. When Tom looked into it, he found that he was sharing his food with the man in the next bed whose employers had abandoned him. Another sick young man secretly shared his food with an elderly mother who depended on him and visited daily to collect her portion.

***

The year 1903 saw an increase in the number of those enquiring about the gospel and an increase in relief work among the poor. Tom saw over 20,000 patients in the dispensaries or in their homes and admitted 243. The workload would have broken most doctors physically but he bore it stoically. In his annual report, he pointed out that the numbers would have been greater if Dr Lillie Saville had not been absent for much of the year. She was the Belgian-trained doctor who delivered the Cochrane twins and she helped with the gynaecological patients.

Tom opened a new dispensary in the South City, which brought the total to five or six, with three small 'hospital' facilities outside the city. His thoughts and plans were constantly leagues ahead of others around him. A wise Chinese proverb says, 'Be not afraid of growing slowly; be afraid only of standing still', and Tom had no intention of doing either. In anticipation of teaching medicine, he lectured at the Methodist University two days a week and taught his assistants in the stables on another two days. The preparation took up entire evenings because no Chinese-language textbooks were available. He translated his lectures into Mandarin and distributed the sheets to his students. Each one took three hours for a clerk to write out.

Opium addicts formed a large part of Tom's practice in the stables. He had already decided that when the hospital opened, he would keep the stables open as a refuge for them. They needed a quiet, secure and peaceful environment. The hospital would admit the better-off patients and those poor people for whom he could afford hospital clothes.

Few if any Western physicians today are exposed to what Tom faced: a combination of extreme drug addiction, grinding poverty, homelessness, malnutrition, disease and limited medical resources. The opium 'sot' (as the Europeans called an addict) was a dreadful sight. He or she was emaciated, jaundiced and watery-eyed, asthmatic, racked by pain and severely constipated. Most addicts had a motion every four or five days and some were bunged up for weeks. They dreaded defaecation, which they described as worse than labour pains. It was often followed by torrential diarrhoea, which had a high mortality rate.

How did missionary doctors treat these poor individuals in those days? If they presented as attempted suicides or with severe overdoses, they underwent stomach wash-outs with permanganate of potash solution. During the first three days they were given two or three grains of opium, but no drugs after that. Their pain and distress were extreme.

On the wall of the refuge attached to a hospital in Soochow an addict wrote, 'While smoking opium we are transported to Paradise. While breaking the opium habit we are tortured in Hell!'

The pain lessened – according to the patients – as the *yin* was drawn out of them. The stock missionary regime included rest, warmth, nutritious fluids, prayers and simple encouragement. Restoring a person this way involved no technology, but it was painstaking work for which many physicians had neither the time nor patience.

How did the patients respond? Tom's notes on treatment are positive but he kept no long-term follow-up. He described one patient who returned to his village where his friends were astonished to learn he had broken the habit. The man went into a shop where people were smoking opium. The wreath of smoke aroused all his old longings and he reached for money to buy a pipeful:

> Then I saw a vision of the hospital ward and a man preaching and
> exhorting me when tempted to trust in the power of Jesus. I lifted my
> heart in prayer for strength and left the shop and escaped the devil's
> snare.

A missionary in another city told a similar good news story as if it was a regular occurrence. A cured addict returned home and greeted his relatives, before throwing the family shrine, the household idols and the ancestral tablets into the courtyard. Panic and dismay! Everyone ran around screaming that he had brought disgrace on the family and that the gods would punish them all. When the matter reached the ears of the mandarin, an enquiry was made and two facts emerged. First, a useless creature who had been at death's door had been miraculously restored to health. Second, whatever magic potion the missionaries had given him had got into the family's water jars, because they too were infected with Christian joy.

However, the evidence from an important report titled *Opinions of Over One Hundred Physicians on the Use of Opium in China* in 1899 is less encouraging.[1] Some conceded that an addict might occasionally be cured in the short term, but insisted that 'long-term cure is as rare

---

[1] The respondents, who were nearly all missionary doctors, had an average of nine years of service in China and two of them had nearly 50 years. See Appendix 2 for details.

as hen's teeth'. Others said they had never seen one case. The overall impression is that lasting cures were rare and involved no more than one to three per cent of cases.

Even so, the missionaries offered some hope and without them the situation would have been far worse. By the 1890s hypodermic syringes had arrived in China and quacks were using them to inject morphine solutions and other powders as 'remedies' for opium addiction. Dr William Park wrote about their activities in Shanghai and Soochow:

> Ghouls with hypodermic syringes and morphine solutions up their sleeves visit the tea shops, giving injections at seven *cash* each. Their victims stand in a row and pass before them, each getting his allowance, like coolies being vaccinated on an emigrant steamer.

The point was that imported morphine (unlike opium) carried no tax so the alleged remedy was cheap. But all that happened was that morphine addiction was substituted for opium addiction, and the injections made things even worse. Needles and syringes were never cleaned, the injection sites got infected and the potential for hepatitis was unlimited. The 1899 report presents a depressing social picture. Addicts were considered untrustworthy, likely to relapse and steal in order to maintain their habit, and incapable of keeping any sort of promise. One missionary concluded that, 'as whisky excites a man to anger, so opium excites him to lying. He is never straightforward and open.' Most missionaries would not allow addicts into church membership, or employ an opium user in their homes for the same reasons. Tom seems to have been more charitable and did not exclude 'cured' addicts from church fellowship.

\*\*\*

The condition of the poor, whether addicts or not, never ceased to wring Tom's heart and he continually looked for ways to relieve their hardships. Often he was unable to help. In December 1903 he turned away a young man because there was no room in the stables and no money to feed him. His only clothing – in bitter winter weather when the Chinese dressed warmly in furs and sheepskins – consisted of torn trousers and a ragged coat. One of his feet, blackened by frostbite and wrapped in rags, was gradually ulcerating off. Whatever *cash* he begged went on a bowl of charcoal which he cradled next to his skin. Tom recounted the conversation. 'I said, "But do you never burn yourself?" "Oh yes!" he replied, and with that he pointed to scars on his skin and holes in his coat where the burning charcoal had dropped.'

Dr Thomas Barnardo, who originally trained to be a medical missionary in China, had a similar experience. One day in the 1870s, there was no room in his shelter in Stepney and he turned away a lad of 11 who later died of exposure and malnutrition. From that day on, the refuge had a sign saying 'No destitute child ever refused admission'.

We do not know what happened to Tom's young man. He finished his report for 1903 for the Home Board with these words:

> The amount of suffering and destitution in this great city is appalling. Hardly a day passes that I do not see tears in the eyes of stolid Christians. One prays and longs for the time that the sick in this great land may be cared for as the sick in our own land are. By embarking on our educational scheme [i.e. the medical college] we are turning our faces towards this goal.

Despite all the obstacles and the discouragement, Tom remembered the old Chinese proverb: 'When you get to the mountains, there will be a way through.'

# 11

## *The Empress and her eunuchs*

After the cholera epidemic, Tom began to attract an altogether different class of patients. Before he came to China, he would have wagered that they existed only in the Arabian Nights tales. But the truth was that in 1901 the Emperor maintained more than 2,000 eunuchs in the Forbidden City. In their heyday under the Ming dynasty there had been between 70,000 and 100,000. Normally they did not venture outside the Forbidden City. The common people called them rats and foxes and invented all manner of stories about them. In the theatre they were portrayed as monsters, and the actors who played them wore female clothes and were caked in make-up.

These men had undergone castration voluntarily. Tom had seen surgical castration (normally unilateral) performed in Glasgow for tumours and vascular conditions. The surrounding anatomy was carefully preserved and the procedure was virtually bloodless. He was appalled to learn what the Chinese did to small boys around ten years old.

A professional called a 'knifer' was called in. After ritually cleansing the skin and invoking the gods, he picked up the genitalia with one hand and used the other to wield a short curved knife. He cut off everything in one drastic sweep, the penis included. Not even a stump was left. Healing took three months and left a scar described as 'the size of a lotus leaf'. When I first read about this practice, I was astonished to learn that the victims did not bleed to death or succumb to infection. Such deaths were apparently rare.

Everything was done with the agreement of the parents and the boy. It was a desperate way out of poverty and starvation. It gave the boy a future in the service of the emperor.

When Tom began to treat members of the imperial family, it was not long before he was asked to treat their eunuchs and so he learned their medical problems. They were neutered as the first flush of puberty approached and immediately after that stricken by the horrors of old age. Dribbling incontinence, damp chronically infected skin, urethral strictures, bladder infections, kidney infections, stones and even cancer awaited them. It was a terrible price to pay and Tom felt great compassion for the sad individuals whom he met in the palace courtyards, dressed in long grey tunics, black trousers and dark blue coats. They walked in small mincing steps, bent forward in a way that made them easily recognizable.

The average Chinese doctor was unable to treat their medical complications. If he could not clear a urinary blockage with a goose quill, he would beat the eunuch with a rod, just as he would pummel the spine of an old woman to drive out her rheumatism. Tom's shiny steel dilators and rubber catheters brought relief to many sufferers, as did his chloroform and aseptic techniques. Soon he was treating dozens of them and discovering things that were in no medical textbook of the day, facts about hot flushes, soft bones and mood changes.

He visited the Forbidden City in the evenings, and when he got home the boys were often in bed. He and Grace would sit drinking tea while he regaled her with his day. She was intrigued by the eunuchs. What were they like as people and what did they do with their time? He told her their lives were hard, and many were addicted to opium and gambling. On a good day they had a kind of serenity but it was quickly upset by small matters. They doted on puppies and songbirds, and burst into tears if one was sick or died. On the other hand, some eunuchs were peevish and harsh. There was a hierarchy with much bullying and unpleasantness.

Several eunuchs had married palace maids whose official title was 'Companions Sitting at Meals' to mark the fact that the relationship was platonic. Some even adopted boys as sons so that ancestor worship would continue without a break. But marriage (Tom observed) did not make eunuchs any happier. They would fly into a temper in a trice with their wives and become very petulant.

As to their work, in other countries they only guarded the harem, but within the Forbidden City they ran the Celestial Palace and did all the manual work. At the top of the pyramid was a chief eunuch whose name was Li Lianying and who came from humble origins.[1] Two rumours circulated about him in the teahouses of Peking. One was that his family was so poor it could not afford a professional castrator so he took a knife and did the job himself. This story was probably an invention to make him look tough, but one or two eunuchs had apparently managed to castrate themselves without bleeding to death.

*Chief Eunuch Li Lianying (right) leading the retinue bearing Empress Dowager Cixi, circa 1903*

The other rumour was a direct contradiction. It said that Li Lianying was so close to the Empress Dowager they must be lovers.

---

[1] For a time he was apprenticed to a cobbler so he was nicknamed P'i Hsiao Li or 'Cobbler's Wax Li'. His official title was Chief Eunuch, which in Chinese is *zongguan taijian*. Some confusion surrounds the office because at any given time there were about ten chief eunuchs in or outside the palace. A less formal title was Favourite Eunuch, and a man could be a favourite eunuch without being a chief eunuch. Li Lianying was both. After the flight of Cixi and the Emperor from Peking in 1900 when he performed them loyal service, he was Cixi's unrivalled favourite and undoubtedly at the top of the hierarchy. I am indebted to Professor N. Kutcher of Syracuse University for these details.

Therefore he must have bribed the castrator and his manhood must be intact. Everyone knew that in her thirties Cixi had a love affair with a handsome young eunuch called Little An. The matter so offended the grandees at court that they had him executed. That was back in 1869.

A weakness in that theory was that Li Lianying would have had to get round the matter of the *bao* or the 'precious'. That was the technical term for the surgical specimen. By law the *bao* had to be pickled and produced before a tribunal whenever a eunuch sought promotion. (This was to provide evidence of his condition, though why he could not be examined on the spot I cannot imagine.) Of course if he were a fraud and did not have a set, he might beg or borrow one.

The medical details are naturally of more interest to a pathologist like myself than to the average reader, but I include them because of their spiritual importance. When a eunuch died his missing parts were placed carefully in the coffin, resting in the appropriate place on the body. Only a man who was physically complete could enter the spirit world, so this was a ruse to fool the guardians of the underworld.

In the end Tom dismissed the rumours about Li Lianying. They were tittle-tattle and only a physical examination could ever establish the truth of the matter. That seemed hardly likely to happen. Tom little dreamed that he would be the man to do it.

\*\*\*

Grace also loved to hear about the Celestial Palace. The language of royalty with its romantic titles and its allusions to heavenly powers fascinated her. Sooner or later the conversation would get round to the Empress Dowager. Occasionally Tom caught a glimpse of the old lady walking slowly in a courtyard with ladies-in-waiting and eunuchs supporting her, but he never met her face to face. One of his patients was a noblewoman who prattled on about the court. She told him that in her good moods Cixi had a magnetic charm, but in her rage she was terrifying. A hairdresser had been executed for botching her coiffure, or so it was said.

*Empress Dowager Cixi (1835–1908) on her throne (Palace Museum, Beijing). A court photo probably taken in 1903 by Yu Xunling, the Empress Dowager's favourite photographer*

*Or so it was said.* Rumours again. Tom had no time for them. In his journal he made occasional observations, describing the Empress Dowager as 'a shrewd and able woman with a consummate skill in statecraft which has probably never been equalled'. He wanted to believe the best of her. He dreamed of a day when he might befriend her and share the good news of Jesus with her. He would not condemn her on the basis of rumours.

Nevertheless, the rumours had been around for a long time. She was only 16 when selected as a concubine in 1851 for the Xianfeng Emperor. That much was true, but from thereon facts struggled with fiction. It was alleged that she smuggled a baby into the palace and passed it off as her own; that she poisoned the Emperor and annihilated all the legitimate regents; that she forced the Empress Zhen to be her co-regent, murdered her own son and made her daughter-in-law commit suicide. Then she illegally appointed her three-year-old nephew to the throne and poisoned Zhen.

She was also accused of causing the naval disaster in the war with Japan in 1894 and of appeasing China's foes. When Emperor Guangxu tried to introduce reforms in 1898, she launched a *coup d'état*, imprisoned him for life and appointed another child, a grand-nephew, as crown prince to justify her third regency. People said she was driven by a hatred of the West and by lust, for she enjoyed orgies with her eunuchs. Her four-and-a-half-inch fingernails were sheathed in gold and jewels which, to European eyes, seemed to symbolize her grasping ambition.

It was a catalogue of cunning, terror and lust and probably some of it was true. Everything at court was corrupt and nobody felt at ease, including Tom. He was far more comfortable in the mules' stables.[2] About Li Lianying he was clearer. As the Favourite Eunuch of the Empress Dowager, his power lay in controlling people's access to her. He was also her private executioner and dispatched a white silk cord to anyone who incurred her displeasure. It was known in Chinese as 'bestowing silk', and meant something quite different from the same phrase in English. It was an invitation to the recipient to avoid the shame of public execution by hanging himself, and it could not be refused.

The Favourite Eunuch remained sitting in Cixi's presence and ate in her chambers, a privilege allowed to nobody else. He advised her on matters of state, which her ministers greatly resented. He was accused of meddling in politics for personal gain. In private he referred to the Empress Dowager and himself as 'we two', a phrase which implied equality. In public he addressed her by her favourite nickname of Lao Foye, 'Venerable Buddha'. It was a play on her title of Holy Mother. In court circles he gave himself the title 'Lord of Nine Thousand Years', which mocked the Emperor's title 'Lord of Ten Thousand Years'. But poor Guangxu had been stripped of his authority and could do nothing about it.

---

[2] Most of the allegations were false or exaggerated, but Europeans believed them. More details about Cixi are given in Appendix 1.

Tom summed up his impressions to Grace. Li Lianying was not a person to cross. He was corrupt and unpredictable – he often failed to do what he had been bribed to do. His apartments were stacked with ill-gotten gains. But he was dedicated to his mistress and if he whispered in her ear, a thing was as good as done. Grace was practical in these matters. If that were the case, she ventured, they needed to pray for the Chief Eunuch. He might be a nasty piece of work, but if Tom was going to touch the throne of China, he needed someone to do a bit of whispering for him.

\*\*\*

Around this time the Cochranes got a new home. A house became vacant in the compound of the London Missionary Society. After the run-down dwelling on the *hutong* it was a great improvement. It was brick-built and had two storeys, an innovation which was not yet accepted in the provinces. It also had an indoor privy and central heating which used hot air piped from the kitchen stove.

The Cochranes now employed a cook, a houseboy and a groom. Their standard of living was comparable with that of a professional family in Edwardian London, but only because things in China were so cheap. And life itself was far less easy. Temperate and tropical diseases occurred together in Peking, and sickness was common amongst the missionary families. Grace kept an eagle eye on her children's health. They still had no *amah*, which she claimed accounted for their robustness.

The compound contained two other houses, a tennis court and an artesian well. The other missionaries in the compound were unmarried so there were no children for the boys to play with. One of the Cochrane twins (Tom Junior) recalled how isolated they felt:

> We did not mix with the Chinese for a variety of reasons. Contact on
> a social level was hardly possible because of the difference in stan-
> dards, culture, hygiene, etc. In any case the well-to-do Chinese did not
> embrace Christianity, nor did they want to associate with foreigners.
> Mother entertained visiting missionaries, visitors interested in mis-
> sionary work and those especially interested in Father's schemes and
> projects. The house was nicknamed The Hotel.

Robert, his twin brother, wrote fondly of his father:

> To us, his family, the memory remains of toil, of buildings being
> erected, of a father who was always busy and yet of a father who, when
> he relaxed, was able to join in the rough and tumble of family games
> that sent us screeching through the house.

Edgar also had warm memories. When he congratulated his father on
his eightieth birthday in 1946, he wrote:

> In childhood the natural bonds of affection between father and son
> were strengthened by the trust your sons had in your skill as a surgeon.
> To our childish minds there appeared to be no ill that did not yield to
> your gentle, healing touch.

A few fragments of handwritten letters from Tom to his boys have survived, enough to show the deep love and affection between them all.

Building began at last on the hospital, but the budget was so tight
that Tom was forced to rethink the project. The plan drawn up in 1903
was for 60 beds, but he had to settle for 30, fewer than the old Free
Healing Hospital, which had 42. And even then it would cost every
penny he had. He wrote to London begging for more funds, but the
Society had its own problems and could do nothing to help. The
dream of a medical school was no closer. The writer Edward Plunkett
wrote, 'Of all the materials for labour, dreams are the hardest and the
artificer in ideas is the chief of workers.' Unless something miraculous
happened soon, this artificer's idea might fade and vanish in the grey
skies over Peking.

# 12

## *Ten Thousand Good Deeds Brought Together*

After the long bitter winter, spring comes to Peking in a rush. In late March Grace would fit her boys into fur coats and mufflers and the next day the temperature might soar ten degrees and they would shed the lot. Grey skies cleared, the ice in the canals melted and the cherry trees broke into blossom. Gardens and courtyards throughout the city turned green with new shoots.

One night around this time in 1903 Tom was wakened by someone banging on the gate of the outer courtyard. He was accustomed to night-time emergencies and so threw on a coat and went to open it. In the moonlight stood an imposing figure in a long coat and behind him a smaller one holding a lantern. A cart stood in the shadows.

The taller man announced himself in a high-pitched voice as Li Li-anying, Favourite Eunuch of the Empress Dowager, and added that he did not have much time. He could only leave the Venerable Buddha when she was asleep. Might he come in?

Tom's heart ran fast as he ushered the man into his study. Had he made a blunder at the palace? Perhaps someone had died. The eunuch's reputation as the Empress Dowager's strong man was unnerving. A word in her ear and Tom would be finished in China; indeed his life might be at risk. But one thing was sure: if Li Lianying was after a bribe he would be disappointed.

The study was simply furnished with an examination couch, a blackwood table and bamboo chairs. The eunuch spotted a relic of Tom's student days on the desk, a plaster model of the human heart. He frowned and said that he hoped it was not real. In China it was a criminal offence to leave organs unburied. He burst out laughing at the look on Tom's face. No, he was joking – he had not come with a silken cord. And he was sorry for the hour, but that was the doctor's doing. He had come because of Tom's remarkable success in treating his colleagues. They sang his praises the whole time.

Without further ceremony he stood and unbuttoned his clothes. At this point it became clear that the rumours of preserved manhood were false. The chief eunuch was neutered indeed and he was suffering like all his kind. His bladder was the size of a melon. As Tom spread a sheet on the examination couch, he remembered the prayer he had made among the ruins of the old hospital. After three long years of waiting, was it about to be answered?

Li Lianying climbed on to the couch without further ado and sat cross-legged like a Buddha. He displayed typical eunuchoid features: smooth hairless skin, rolls of fat and enlarged breasts. He wore a large cotton pad under his robe. A whiff of urine arose which the fragrance of jasmine could not mask. Tom remembered a popular phrase, 'as smelly as a eunuch'. The Chinese claimed they could smell one at a hundred yards.

Tom asked a few questions before getting him to lie flat for the examination. As he expected, he found a urethral stricture that had been exacerbated by clumsy attempts to stretch it. Now it was causing urinary retention and an infection. He selected a catheter and explained what he was going to do.

At first Li Lianying lay quietly while Tom tried to pass the instrument, but it proved difficult and the man's face began to glisten with sweat and his breath came in grunts. He was in such a state that he made no objection to Tom's laughing gas, and after a few lungfuls the job was done. Tom helped him into a chair and apologized for hurting him. Would His Excellency care for tea while he recovered? It would be an honour to serve him. That was most kind, Li Lianying remarked, but could he not send a servant? Tom explained that the Cochranes lived simply. The only servant who lived with them was away.

Now with his bladder comfortably empty and his pain receding, Li Lianying was in no hurry to leave. He sipped the tea and talked about life at court in the genteel language used by courtiers. He described the whims of his mistress and the demands she made upon him, but without resentment and always with respect. He laughed a great deal, making patterns in the air with an ivory fly whisk and displaying a fortune in gold teeth.

Listening to him, Tom found it hard to believe that this affable man could have poisoned or drowned hundreds of victims. Or that he had sided with the Boxers and was complicit in the deaths of many Christians. He remembered what the eunuch said about leaving his mistress only when she slept. Was Her Highness aware that he was here?

Li Lianying smiled. Surely the doctor knew that the Celestial Palace was full of spies. How could one keep a secret from the Venerable Buddha? Of course she knew he was here. She was like a mother to him, caring for his health and happiness.

That was convenient, said Tom, because he needed to come again to complete the treatment. The eunuch agreed, but it must be at nighttime, for political reasons of course. Tom agreed. Meanwhile the eunuch must drink only fluids that would turn the urine acidic. Strong tea was good but the juice of cranberries was better.

He took out his pen to write a list, reflecting that only God could have brought about this meeting. He once caused a religious leader to visit Jesus in the dead of night so that each could speak his mind without interruption. But Tom had to be careful; one thoughtless remark might drive this Nicodemus away.

Li Lianying was intrigued by Tom and asked many questions. Why had he come to China? Why on earth did he work among the beggars, pedlars and opium devils? Would he not be wealthy and respected in England? Tom was vague in his answers. Soft and slow, that was the way. The eunuch stayed for an hour and left after agreeing to return in two days' time. The next morning Tom received a beautiful porcelain vase and a note inscribed with the Chinese ideogram meaning 'With friendship'.

\*\*\*

When Tom went over the visit in his mind, he felt uncomfortable. Li Lianying had been friendly enough, but he had blood on his hands, the blood of Christians. How should he deal with such a man? Indeed, should he deal with him at all? Dr Li took a different view. He reminded Tom that he had done nothing to make the meeting happen. All he had done was to pray for three years to touch the throne. In the same way he had not asked to meet Prince Su and he certainly did not create a cholera epidemic to do so. These things happened, and if God chose to use evildoers for his purposes, it was not for believers to object. It should be marvellous in their eyes.

Next time, Dr Li said, the eunuch would invite him to petition the throne. It was standard practice. And if the Venerable Buddha listened to her Favourite Eunuch, she would not refuse him.

When Li Lianying arrived for his second appointment he was as friendly as ever. Tom plucked up courage to ask about his castration and he was happy to talk about it. Yes (he boasted), it was his handiwork. His family in Chihli province had been as poor as temple mice and lived on millet and tea made from tree bark. He was the third son, and the only way to escape starvation was to become a eunuch and enter the imperial service. His family did not even have the money for the operation.

Tom had to say something. He murmured that whatever His Excellency had done must have required much courage.

The eunuch replied that ignorant people had no idea what a desperate man would do. They thought that procreation was a man's strongest urge. That was not true – it was hunger. Who in their right mind would value his manhood over his life, especially if there was a chance of living a comfortable existence with a full belly?

Tom cast an eye over the puckered scar. It was as neat as he had seen, not an amateur job. He remarked quietly that he knew something about desperation. When he worked in Inner Mongolia, the people had no food and no hope. They wore rags and ate cattle fodder. Live babies were thrown on the rubbish tip every day. Many had collapsed and died in his dispensary from starvation, not disease.

The eunuch's eyes widened; he had not heard about Tom's work in Chaoyang. He listened as the doctor described what Western medicine had achieved – the babies saved, the barren become fertile, the cripples walking and the blind seeing.

Tom warmed to his theme. China was the sick man of Asia, but its sickness was more than political. The country was ravaged by illnesses and infectious diseases which the Europeans had long since learned to control. An ocean of misery could be avoided if the Chinese were taught elementary hygiene, sewage disposal, nutrition, how to control harmful insects and animals, how to deal with epidemics, and so on.

Li Lianying listened gravely and appeared to agree. But, he said, China already had too many mouths to feed and they kept multiplying. Maybe an occasional famine or epidemic was not a bad thing.

Tom knew the Malthusian argument and he avoided the quick retort. The best reply was that China would only achieve its potential as a nation if it had a healthy, well-fed population with a full life expectancy. That was the key not only to personal happiness but also to the prosperity and stability of the empire. Secure those for China, and the Peach Blossom Spring would flower again. Finally he talked about the grain shop and stables where he worked within sight of the Forbidden City, surrounded by the evils he was desperate to cure: disease, poverty and despair. Every morning the city's streets and canals contained the bodies of men and women for whom nobody cared. They were just left to die.

At this Li Lianying raised an eyebrow and observed that no nation had a monopoly on compassion, least of all the British. He waved an imaginary opium pipe in the air and mockingly inhaled from it. Then he smiled and added that he knew the good doctor was not complicit in the foreign smoke. Indeed people said that he actually treated addicts, surely a most thankless task. So would he please explain: what drove him to these good deeds? From where did all this extraordinary concern for others come?

It was the invitation of which every evangelist dreams. As Tom applied the ointment he talked about Jesus Christ, a name that the eunuch had never heard except as a curse. He described the Great Physician who shattered every concept people had about caring for one other. Jesus brought not only physical healing but also love and forgiveness to everyone, and he taught them to show the same love and forgiveness to others. In this he showed that body, soul and spirit were inseparable. It was not possible to focus on the spirit and ignore the rest.

The eunuch stroked his beardless cheek. Focusing on the spirit was precisely what the Eastern faiths did. They elevated the spirit to the detriment of the body and in so doing minimized the importance of relieving pain and suffering.

Tom continued with his theme. Jesus loved men and women of every race, especially the poor, the disabled and the outcasts. He loved eunuchs too. They were mentioned several times in the Bible with respect and care. He taught that every life was precious to God. That was why the only places on earth where the sick were cared for properly were places where Jesus was worshipped. Had the eunuch heard of the missionary hospital in Hankow? They called it 'The Hospital of Universal Love'.

To Li Lianying these were uncomfortable ideas; no one who preached them would last long in the Forbidden City. But he could see what made Tom Cochrane so passionate, apparently in love with all of China. How different he was from other foreigners! And Tom's description of the suffering of the *nongmin* probably reminded him of his origins and the price he had paid to escape them.

Sensing the moment had arrived, Tom described his dream of training thousands of Chinese students in Western medicine. He spoke of uniting the missionary societies for that purpose and how he had perfected his Mandarin in order to teach and to translate. He spoke of the need for nurses and midwives and for public health programmes and vaccination programmes to eradicate diseases. He spoke of cleansing the capital and giving it decent sanitation and clean water. The ideas came tumbling out.

When he finished, the eunuch was silent for a while. Yes, times were changing, he said finally, and the throne might be favourable to these ideas. After the Boxer Uprising, the Venerable Buddha had retained her position by a hair's breadth and she was making efforts to be friends with the West. Reforms in the legal and educational systems were in the air and she had abolished *lingchi*, or 'death by a thousand cuts'. She even hosted tea parties at the Celestial Palace for diplomats' wives. Tom knew this, but he also knew that at heart the regime was unchanged. Above all, no discussion of Christianity was permitted at court.

At the door the eunuch's parting remark was as Li Hsiao Ch'uan had predicted: 'Dr Cochrane, petition the throne. Do it at once and I will add my voice and urge Her Majesty to approve it. I cannot guarantee the outcome but I shall do what I can.' There was no hint that he expected the customary 'favour' in return.

\*\*\*

Making a petition to the throne was an unprecedented step for a foreigner to take and the procedure was complicated. The request had to be drawn up in archaic language, and the fact that Tom was seeking not just approval but also financial support made it doubly difficult. He decided to take his problem to a patient who was also a friend, the Grand Councillor Yehenala Natong, a Manchu minister of the same family lineage as the Empress Dowager. Though not a Christian, he sympathized with Tom's ideas on China's health. It also helped that in 1903 Natong was Minister of Revenue.

Protocol made it almost impossible for people to see imperial ministers uninvited. They waited for days for an appointment and even then were obliged to sit in an anteroom for hours. The ambassadors of the Great Nations usually took a good book along with them to pass the time. To Tom's surprise he was ushered in immediately; Natong rose and embraced him, an unusual gesture for the Chinese. He had tears in his eyes. It was a difficult week, he explained. His honourable mother was failing – the time had come for her to mount the Dragon and ascend to the Nine Springs. Earlier that day he had informed the foreign legations that he would be in mourning for the customary 100 days.

Tom offered to see the old lady immediately. When he examined her, he diagnosed pneumonia, but happily the crisis had already passed. He prescribed medicine and fluids and gave the servants instructions on how to look after her.

Later that day he visited his 'place of thunder' in the Western Hills. It was not far from a monastery once visited by the eighteenth-century Qianlong Emperor, who had a reputation as a poet. On a granite slab are inscribed his words:

Why have I sought this dizzy height, why sought this mountain den?
I tread as on enchanted ground, unlike the abode of men.
Beneath my feet my realm I see, as in a map unrolled,
Above my head a canopy, bedecked with clouds of gold.

It was evening, and when the sun dropped below the horizon the clouds did indeed turn russet-gold. A breeze stirred the pine trees, making the branches vibrate like harps. Tom felt the same peace flowing through him as when he first prayed for Mongolia to be won for Christ. Something was shifting in the heavenly realms.

To the astonishment of everyone except Tom, the old lady recovered and showed every intention of living for many more years. Natong gratefully drew up the petition and presented it to the throne. Others helped behind the scene: Sir Ernest Satow, the new British minister in Peking; Dr Douglas Gray, the physician at the British legation; and of course Sir Robert Hart. When the Empress Dowager's decision was announced on 26 May 1903, she not only approved the request but also donated 10,000 ounces of silver towards the college. It was the first gift of its kind in China's history. In today's terms it was worth around £150,000. George Morrison, the *Times* correspondent in Peking, cabled the news home. Within 24 hours all the London newspapers carried it.

That was only the beginning. At the court a subscription list was opened for the great and the good to follow Cixi's example. Their gifts poured into the London Missionary Society's account and added another 10,000 taels. A petition to the emperor resulted in the gift of a piece of land adjacent to the site that Tom had purchased. Supporters of the London Missionary Society also contributed. By the time the medical college opened, over 62,000 taels of silver had been raised.

To commemorate this generosity, Tom commissioned a subscription book, of which a copy survives at the School of Oriental and African Studies in London. It is beautifully covered in silk and titled *Ten Thousand Good Deeds Brought Together*. It outlines the purpose of the medical college and the need for funds. It records the names of the provincial governors, government officials and departments that contributed, as well as the Chinese and Western taipans, businesses, shop owners and private individuals who made donations.

And so the Empress Dowager Cixi allowed the first Western medical school to be built in Peking, in the knowledge it was going to be built and run by missionaries. The irony is that five years earlier she would as gladly have let the Boxers chop their heads off.

# 13

## *Getting started*

In his annual report of 1905 to the London Missionary Society, Tom apologized for its brevity, confessing that it was 'the busiest year of my life'. He added, 'I have been so weighed down with work and responsibilities that I feel as if I had done nothing well.'

The business of the hospital and the medical school could have filled every waking minute. There were committee meetings, site meetings, curriculum meetings, negotiations with city authorities, contracts to be written and subscription lists to be supervised. At the same time his clinical workload increased to 23,787 consultations. It left little time for evangelism. He was learning the hard truth that (as he put it), 'Medical colleges are costly to build, costly to equip, costly to run and difficult to staff efficiently!' Staffing was a particular problem. Cross-cultural teaching demands a higher teacher–student ratio than conventional teaching. In addition, the attrition rate from sickness, the lack of printed resources and the need for regular furlough meant that he needed more staff than first calculated.

Where would he find a super-breed of medical educators who were fluent in Mandarin and acquainted with Chinese culture? It was not a question of money; there were no such academics to be found in Britain or America. The only Westerners capable of teaching medicine in Mandarin were missionary doctors like himself. And that meant he had to obtain the agreement of the senior ordained men who oversaw the stations. Their societies had a critical role to play.

When he first met these reverend gentlemen soon after the Boxer Uprising, they baffled him. Looking back 50 years later, he wrote:

> When I went to the city of Peking at the beginning of this century, I found four missionary societies under four different Chinese names

which were incomprehensible to the Chinese. To my astonishment
they never met together to co-ordinate their work.

Their priority was their own interests which they defended as zeal-
ously as any mandarin. In practice this meant that for most of the
time they ignored each other. Jesus' injunction to his disciples to bear
one another's burdens might apply in Shanghai and Canton but not
in Peking.

A divided Christendom was confusing to a Chinese person. One
convert asked Tom for an explanation. Why all these strange names
and labels? In China one temple did not stand against another, and
people were free to worship at many different shrines. You could be
a Buddhist one week, a Taoist the next, and still follow Confucius.
Why did Christians not feel the same way? Tom tried to explain that
all the missionaries loved Jesus and wanted to spread the good news
throughout China. They were all on the same side. But his questioner
persisted: which was the true Church of Jesus Christ because that
was the one he wanted to join. Was it the Meyi Meihui (American
Methodist Church) or the Lundun Hui (London Missionary Society)
Church?

Tom could only shrug and say they were all true. When he tried
to explain the English word 'denominations', the man laughed. What
a strange word. It sounded as if it had *demons* in it. Remembering
Scotland's history of church divisions, Tom may have been tempted
to agree. 'Why do we have this rivalry?' he asked Grace later. 'Four
hundred million Chinese need the gospel. That's more than enough
to go around.'

One solution might have been to give the female missionaries some
authority; married and unmarried, they outnumbered the men and
they could have shaken things up. But mission work was still a man's
world. A few years earlier, an American Baptist conference had affirmed that 'Women's work in the foreign field must be careful to
recognize the headship of men.'

The matter of the churches worried Tom greatly. It was not just
a question of avoiding wrangling over doctrine; there must be true
oneness. If the Westerners could not teach a harmonious, undivided
Protestant faith to young Chinese students, the future of the gospel

was uncertain. In his first winter in Peking he formed a plan that went a step beyond the medical college. It was for the missionary societies to come together and create a body that would further tertiary education in north-east China, including science, literature, medicine and theology. The idea was that it would form the basis of a new university.

He read a paper on these lines to the Peking Missionary Association and began with these words: 'Gentlemen, I believe that in China we must not preach sectarian Christianity and the concept of a particular church, but the broad idea of the kingdom of the Father.' The audience went quiet; this was radical stuff. He pressed on. Why could there not be one Church of Christ in China? It was a simple step to drop the foreign names and titles which the Chinese did not understand anyway. They were not interested in sectarian differences. That was how the early Church grew in the New Testament and it turned the world upside down.

He concluded with a prophecy that resonates in our own troubled times: 'Give China our scientific secrets without our Christianity, and we shall have raised up a dragon of portentous size and strength, a competitor without scruple or conscience, and woe betide the rest of mankind!'

The initial reception was cool but Tom persevered. He organized a conference at which many misunderstandings were cleared up. One missionary proposed that throughout China every street chapel should be called Fu Yin Tang, 'Good News Hall', and known only by its street. Similarly each church which held Sunday services should be called Li Pai Tang, 'Worship Hall', and be known by its town or village. Tom seized on the idea and wrote to every Protestant missionary in China. (There were several hundreds so it was a lot of writing.)

Tom and his colleagues never succeeded in doing away with denominations throughout northern China; it was a miracle too far. But in some places, including Peking and Tientsin, an astonishing degree of what was called 'missionary comity' (defined as courtesy and considerate behaviour) developed. By 1913 Tom could write that there was practically one church in Tientsin. Chinese

Christians were delighted at anything that drew the denominations together.[1]

In Peking the desire to develop higher education and to make it Christian caught on. The four societies wrangled (as was their custom) for months over names, but eventually they formed a body called the Union Committee to oversee departments for arts, sciences, theology and medicine. Tom was appointed head of the medical department. Since the London Missionary Society had an excellent reputation for medical work, they agreed that it should have the task of establishing a medical school.

In this roundabout way Tom had secured the promise of medical missionaries as lecturers and tutors for his college, and it happened long before he had the money to start building. The runners were on the blocks before the starting gun was loaded, and everyone was pleased with what had been achieved. The societies even agreed on a name: the Union Medical College (often abbreviated to UMC).

\*\*\*

Building the hospital, which for a time was known as the Lockhart Hospital, began first. The plan for half a hospital was scrapped and the original plan reinstated. The site which Tom had purchased was off Hatamen Street, a spacious avenue which ran from north to south and was named after a fourteenth-century Mongol prince called Hada. Tom bought it with money from the Boxer Indemnity. It covered approximately ten acres and was adequate for both the hospital and the college.

It was close to the Ketteler memorial, a large and unsightly marble archway erected in memory of the German diplomat murdered by the Boxers in 1900. This was designed on the lines of a traditional Chinese *paifang* (arch) with Gothic touches. The German government insisted on it and the Chinese had to pay for it. They did so with a bad grace.

---

[1] The call for a united Chinese Church grew in later years. The modern concept of ecumenicism is said to have been born at the Edinburgh World Missionary Conference in 1910, and the China Continuation Committee continued its vision in China. In 1927 the Church of Christ in China was established as a non-denominational movement with significant Chinese involvement.

For years the rickshaw men (the taxi drivers of the day) told European tourists, 'This is the memorial to honour the man who killed Baron von Ketteler.' It was removed by French and Italian troops three days after the armistice in November 1918.

One of the last cases that Tom treated in the stables was a 19-year-old lama from Mongolia who was blinded by cataracts. He was one of four brothers and tradition dictated that the eldest become a lama. He was chosen against his will, as he lamented to Tom:

> My lot is a hard one. I do not believe in Buddhism, I am not allowed
> to marry and I am required to give up all my friends and live in the
> temple. The oldest lama there knows nothing about the soul so in
> addition to my physical darkness I am in spiritual darkness also.

Tom operated and restored his sight. Then something wonderful happened. The young man vowed he would never go back to the monastery again. 'I have not only got back my sight – light has entered my soul. I want to become a Christian.'

\*\*\*

The teaching hospital opened early in 1906, a little ahead of the medical school. With the wards open, Tom was now able to admit people of means and to perform complex surgical operations. This produced problems of etiquette; for example, it was not proper for a foreign male doctor to operate on a high-born lady. That was the dilemma that faced him with Duchess Te, the wife of a nephew of the Empress Dowager who was also her favourite lady-in-waiting. A small dumpy woman, she needed what Tom described as 'a serious and difficult' gynaecological operation. She summoned up the nerve to attend the hospital, but there her courage deserted her. She knew her behaviour would stir up trouble at court and she panicked. At this point Tom called in Grace to calm her down and the two women hit it off. The Duchess proposed an ingenious solution. There and then she 'adopted' Grace as her sister, which meant that Tom became her brother-in-law. That changed the situation altogether.

The operation was performed under general anaesthetic by Tom and Dr Li. Afterwards Empress Dowager Cixi demanded a series of medical bulletins. When the Duchess returned to the palace, she was summoned by Cixi, who seethed with curiosity. What was this sleeping medicine? Did it really allow a woman to be cut open, have her organs removed and be sewn up without knowing what she had lost? *It did?*[2]

The Duke (who was clearly fond of his wife) wrote to Tom:

> Your skill is truly greater than our most famous doctors of antiquity, whose names have been held in esteem for generations. When you stretched forth your hands, the disease gradually disappeared; it was springtime with your patient and health and peace returned. Now I cannot find words to thank you for your goodness.

Cixi expressed her pleasure and instructed her nephew to make a generous donation to Tom's subscription fund.

*Court photograph, 1906, showing Tom and Grace Cochrane with the Duke and Duchess of Te, by the Japanese photographer Sanshichiro Yamamoto. The Cochrane boys are centre. Left to right are Tom Junior, Edgar and Robert*

Cochrane Family Collection

---

[2] Cixi's line of questioning suggests that the operation was either a hysterectomy or removal of an ovary. Either was a major procedure in 1906.

With Cixi's permission, photographs were taken. One is a group picture of the two families, the Cochranes and the Tes, with their children. The Cochrane boys are in Edwardian suits, Grace wears fur and a regally flowered hat, and Tom looks awkward in a top hat, stiff collar and morning dress. He would joke about it in later years but he always gave the credit to Grace. Neither of them quite got over the fact that they were adopted as members of the imperial Chinese family.

\*\*\*

Tom always had a prodigious capacity for work. He now had a practice divided between the nobility, the eunuchs, the hospital and the dispensaries. He was soon to be principal and professor of anatomy at the Union Medical College and a surgeon at the Lockhart Hospital (though he gladly yielded the post of senior surgeon when Thomas Stuckey FRCS (Fellow of the Royal College of Surgeons) arrived). He was medical adviser to the Chinese government and various legations and he had established a language school on the hospital premises which enabled new missionaries to learn Mandarin. These were remarkable achievements for a man who never obtained – or sought – a single postgraduate qualification.

On 29 December, in his last diary entry for 1905, he prayed:

> Help me to prepare and deliver sermons in Chinese. Help me to make the spiritual part of the college work a success. Help me to make the college the best in China, the hospital the best in Peking, and oh! help me above all, to hasten the time.

The next few pages are missing and one can only imagine the pressures under which Tom was working. Fortunately the building of the college was well done by a Chinese contractor who took a great interest in the project and made only a small profit. The buildings were impressive and met with general approval. Tom allowed himself a moment of satisfaction and wrote, 'The result is something to be grateful for and is unique in the history of missions in China.'

However, drawing up the curriculum for a Chinese medical degree proved difficult. A problem which I have already mentioned was the rarity of medical books written in Chinese. The difficulty was that the technical vocabulary did not exist. To the Chinese a bone was a bone; why bother to give different names to nearly 300 of them in the human body? In anatomy, pathology, pharmacology and physiology, thousands of new words had to be created. The China Medical Missionary Society, which was established in 1886, had set up a nomenclature committee to fill the gaps, but it was numbingly slow work because everything had to be evaluated and agreed.

But the Chinese had a saying that 'a good teacher is better than a barrowful of books' and Tom was by now a linguist capable of creating his own ideograms for words which did not exist in Chinese. Soon he was tackling *Heath's Anatomy*, thus translating one of the world's most difficult subjects into one of its most difficult languages. It was published in Mandarin in 1909 and was followed by his translation of *Heath's Osteology* in 1910. Tom was now so fluent that his Chinese friends agreed that if five people were talking with the excellent doctor, you could not tell which one was the foreigner.

***

One night in 1906, when Tom was hard at work at a translation, Grace came into his study, her face bright with pleasure. 'There's someone outside you'll be glad to see!' By the door stood a young man grasping a bag and twisting his cap in his hands. He was taller and sturdier than Tom remembered.

'Liu-i, by all that's wonderful!' It was six years since they had parted under a night sky lit by the glare of burning buildings. They talked for hours and Liu-i told how he had carried on Tom's work after the Boxers were driven off. He had little equipment and he made many mistakes, yet people came to him because they trusted him and had nowhere else to turn.

Tom wrote:

> On that moonlit night, standing under an almond tree, he told me of the number of lives he had saved by what I had taught him. And then, lifting his face to heaven and with deep emotion, he prayed for me in words that inspired me.

There was news of patients and church members, of deaths, marriages and births, as well as messages of goodwill. Tom was touched to know that he was not forgotten.

Liu-i had come to Peking to see if he had a chance of being admitted to the college. Tom thumped him in the back and told him, yes, there was every chance! The request summarized everything he had prayed for. If this young man were trained in medicine he would return to Chaoyang and the people would have their own doctor, capable of doing all that Tom had done. The wheel would turn full circle.

Liu-i was one of 200 young men who applied for a place at the college. They were drawn from all over China, from as far north as Mukden and as far south as Foochow (Fuzhou) 1,500 miles away. They sat a stiff examination and only the top 50 were accepted. The lad from Chaoyang was among them and he graduated as a doctor in 1911.

# 14

## *Years of fulfilment*

The Union Medical College was so named because of the collaboration of six missionary societies.[1] The opening on 13 February 1906 celebrated their unity with Chinese pomp and circumstance. Tom had asked for an imperial deputation. 'A bold bid for a great boon,' he called it and he got his wish.

For two and a half centuries the Manchus used processions and parades to create awe among the Han Chinese. They dazzled them with their ceremonies and military power, just as they paralysed them with their cruelty. The route from the Forbidden City to the college was barricaded and the shops and restaurants were decorated with banners. Soldiers lined the streets as the procession set off. One of the teaching staff wrote (and it was probably no exaggeration), 'Seldom have so many Chinese high officials and representatives of so many Great Powers been assembled together.' Two imperial princes in yellow-banded sedan chairs led the procession with riders on horseback and marching retinues, followed by dukes in red-banded chairs. Next came the lesser nobility and government officials including the ministers and deputy ministers for war, education, finance and foreign affairs. The cream of the diplomatic corps in their morning dress followed in sedan chairs.

The guests crowded into the college's lecture hall, which accommodated 350 people, to hear speeches in Chinese and English. Grand Councillor Natong opened the proceedings in his court regalia. He described Tom Cochrane as 'a gentleman eminent in his profession, who

---

[1] They were the London Missionary Society, the Church of England Mission (Society for the Propagation of the Gospel), the American Presbyterian Mission, the American Board of Commissioners for Foreign Mission, the London Medical Missionary Association and the American Methodist Episcopal Mission. The 'union' appellation had been used by societies collaborating elsewhere, but the idea was new in Peking.

spared no pains in carrying through his project to a successful issue'. One day, he said, the college would become an instrument of incalculable benefit. Its fame would spread throughout the Chinese Empire.

Tom's patron Sir Robert Hart went further. He predicted that students at the college would make scientific discoveries of worldwide importance. No country valued education more than China (this was debatable, in view of its infinitesimal literacy rate) and it was only a matter of time before the college received regular government support. Tom breathed an amen.

Later there were guided tours. In the foyer the guests passed a number of exhibits in glass cases which Tom had placed there to gauge their reactions. Would they take offence? Would they assume that the bones were from victims murdered in the cause of science? Syphilitic femurs might have provoked a riot in the provinces, but not in Hatamen Street. The tour ended up in the library where tea and cakes were being served in polite English fashion by the missionaries' wives.

\*\*\*

*The main block of the Union Medical College on Hatamen Street,*
*Peking, newly opened in 1906*
Cochrane Family Collection

MEMBERS OF THE TEACHING STAFF PRESENT AT THE GRADUATION CEREMONY.

| | Mr. Biggin. | Dr. Mullowney. | Mr. Read. | |
| Dr. Cormack. | | Dr. Stenhouse. | Dr. Stuckey. | Dr. Dilley. |
| Dr. Wheeler. | Dr. Hall. | Dr. Hopkins. | Dr. Cochrane. | Dr. Peill. | Dr. Young. |

*Academic staff of the Union Medical College in 1911. They are all missionary doctors. Tom Cochrane is seated, centre right*

Author's collection

The Union Medical College got off to a flying start, with a faculty of eight British and American doctors, supported by visiting lecturers. In the second year they grew to a dozen. One of them was Ernest Peill, a young Edinburgh graduate who got his FRCS in 1901 and served for eight years on the staff. He observed that, 'Cochrane long ago determined to make the college the best in China and he will stick at no sacrifice to accomplish his end. It is no mere hobby with him, but a divine commission.'

Things did not always run smoothly, partly because of Tom's leadership style. Norman Goodall, who wrote the second volume of the two-part history of the London Missionary Society, described him as living 'a life of constructive restlessness. He always sought for agreement, but if it was slow in coming he never flinched from stepping

153

out and leading the way.' A colleague put it rather less charitably: 'It is difficult to argue with a man who has a sense of divine vocation.'

We should remember that by birth and temperament Tom was a Victorian, and a Scot to boot. He believed in hard work, discipline and thrift. His sense of discipline and authority was reflected in the nickname which the medical students gave him: Ta Lung, 'the Great Dragon'. (It certainly did not refer to his size, because he was below the height of the average European.)

In July 1906 the thorny question of professional recognition was settled. The Imperial Board of Education authorized the college to hold examinations and confer degrees endorsed with the words, 'established with imperial sanction and registered with the Imperial Board of Education'. Later it forbade anyone other than traditional doctors from practising medicine without a valid qualification.

The life of the medical students was not unlike that of English public schoolboys. They slept in dormitories in a block designed by a firm of English architects in Tientsin and ate together in a canteen or prepared their own food. For those like Liu-i who had been brought up in mud villages, a two-storey building with electricity, glass windows and hot and cold running water was more an epiphany than a culture shock. He had never seen a tap or a toilet.

Three missionaries, Drs Wenham, Wheeler and Stenhouse, were house tutors. They shared a study, a dining room and a sitting room. It was a big advantage to have teachers living in the same building as the students, but finances were so tight that they were required to pay rent for the privilege.

The first year covered anatomy, physiology, histology and therapeutics. A problem arose immediately with anatomy. Dissections are essential to teach students how the body works, just as post-mortem examinations are essential to see how diseases spread through them. Post-mortems also inform the clinicians whether their diagnosis and treatment have been correct. Even today the causes of death which general practitioners and hospital doctors write on death certificates are often erroneous or incomplete. The figure often quoted in my day for such mistakes was up to 30 per cent of cases.

Ancestor worship in China demanded reverence for the dead, and any kind of dissection had been banned for centuries. It was called the 'custom of four thousand years'. Even in cases of murder a post-mortem examination was not permitted, because it would prevent the victim from entering into the spirit world. If a foreign doctor performed even a partial autopsy, his or her life might be forfeit.[2]

When Tom asked Chinese doctors what they knew of anatomy, he was shown carved ivory manikins in which the internal organs (including some that did not exist) were arranged in curious ways. For instance the stomach lay within the chest alongside the heart and lungs with no clue as to how they were related to each other. The liver had seven lobes, not four; a mysterious addition called 'the Gate of Life' was located between the kidneys; and the pancreas was conspicuous by its absence. In one ancient diagram the oesophagus was shown passing through the heart and thence to the liver and the stomach.

In the face of this ignorance, the anatomy demonstrators at Union Medical College did the best they could with lantern slides, *papier mâché* models, charts and bones. They sewed socks together to represent intestines and where possible used animal tissues, but none of this was ideal.

During the first term, the 'custom of four thousand years' provided Tom with the fright of his life. He was making his rounds one evening when he noticed a glow in the cellar of the students' residence. He went to investigate and discovered a medical student in a long black gown and pigtail bending over a stove. A human head was bobbing around in boiling water and the student was stirring it with a pair of chopsticks. He was terrified by the principal's sudden appearance and stutteringly confessed that he had raided a graveyard and dug up a body. He had severed the head and smuggled it into the college and now he was boiling off the flesh. 'Good specimens are so scarce,' he pleaded pitifully. Mercifully the affair did not leak out and Tom did not speak of it for years. In 1913 the problem of dissections was solved by a change in the law, as we shall see.

In addition to lectures and clinics, the students attended morning and evening prayers, which were led alternately by them and their teachers. Tom held weekly Bible classes and there were YMCA

---

[2] This was in China proper. In Hong Kong, a crown colony with a population of less than half a million, the medical officer of health authorized about 2,000 examinations a year, an astonishingly high figure.

meetings. Three missionaries taught language classes in the evening to improve whatever English the students had. On Sundays they were encouraged to visit dispensaries in villages outside Peking to practise dispensing and bandaging and to preach. After less than two years Ernest Peill wrote, 'Quite a number of students have made their debut as a preacher and a large number of people have had the gospel presented to them in a fresh and attractive setting.'

These were vigorous, high-spirited young men, like the characters in Rudyard Kipling's book *Stalky and Co.*, and they needed fun and relaxation. Unless a dust storm happened to be in progress, they played football three times a week on a field belonging to the Belgian legation, pigtails flying in all directions. The presence of a referee and a leather ball were novelties and made them play seriously. From the touchline Tom noted, 'They have improved considerably since the beginning of term, though they are still rather unmindful of the rules and regulations.'

They also did physical drill to keep fit and they made good use of the tennis courts. Again the similarity with minor English public schools like Eltham College, where missionaries sent their sons, is obvious.

In 1907 the Union Medical College played a football match against the Imperial University which they lost one–nil. It was just as well, because at that time it had 50 students and the university had 300. To win would have caused a serious loss of face. On another occasion some of Tom's students attended a government sports day at which UMC was the only Christian college among a gathering of 20,000.

The students had a keen sense of vocation. They were China's first generation of scientifically trained doctors, a privilege that was well worth a sacrifice. When a new lecturer came out from Britain or America they welcomed him with a song they composed in English to show their appreciation:

> The healing art in other lands
> Widens its scope from day to day.
> And China dark and dismal stands
> With scarce a single brightening ray.
> Grudge not to leave your home and friends,
> Till truth has reached unto the world's ends.

\*\*\*

Meanwhile the clinical workload at the Lockhart teaching hospital grew rapidly. According to the first annual report, the missionary doctors treated 40,000 patients, 482 of them as in-patients; 255 underwent operations under general anaesthetic. Most of the consultations were located in the new hospital, with a small number in a women's hospital in the East City for which the London Mission Society was responsible. It also oversaw dispensaries in the West City and in villages up to ten miles outside Peking.

Almost before the paint was dry in the corridors, the hospital had to borrow classrooms from the college and turn them into extra wards. Fortunately there was room for expansion, thanks to Tom's foresight. Land in Peking was getting expensive and the large plot that he had bought with indemnity money was already worth three times what he paid. But finding the money for more building work was another thing. In his report to the London Missionary Society, the senior surgeon Thomas Stuckey complained that its annual grant was an eighth of what the American Missionary Society gave its hospital, and the Lockhart had a far greater workload. The Society's grant did not even pay for the hospital's coal, and in 1906–7 was unable to give anything.

It was a great frustration to Tom, who had ambitious plans to build a tuberculosis sanatorium in the Western Hills, a nursing home for incurable diseases, an asylum for the mentally ill and a residence for the college principal; the list went on and on. Always the pioneer, he was constantly seeking horizons beyond the present.

The medical staff was encouraged to take on legation appointments and fundraising activities to help pay the bills. But it was done at a cost. Ernest Peill wrote, 'We have no objection to hard work, but our time and strength being limited we have to neglect our proper missionary work in order to raise funds to support it, just as the apostles of old had to neglect their preaching to serve tables.' He had little energy left for his evening sessions with a Chinese language tutor.

Tom constantly had to remind everyone that the college had been a venture of faith from the beginning. And he constantly brought its needs before God. A diary entry on 30 May 1907 reads:

> I want to be right with Thee, my Father, from centre to circumference, in money matters, in time for devotion and family affairs, in studies

and the spending of my time . . . I would like to be a millionaire, my
Father, for Thy work. Oh, give me money!

God never made Tom a millionaire. At just the right time he provided
a better way.[3]

\*\*\*

In the nineteenth century Peking's mediaeval police force was well
known for its corruptness and inefficiency. After the Boxer Uprising
it was modernized and the new recruits showed an admirable dedica-
tion to their work. This prompted one of the doctors to write with a
touch of sarcasm, 'When the small official ceases to extort bribes, and
subordinates even his own life to the good of the public, the time of
China's redemption is evidently drawing near.'

The injured citizens whom the police brought to the hospital in
1906 included the victims of a cinema explosion (which made the
Imperial Court panic, thinking a revolution had started), workers
rescued from burning railway sheds, a man plucked from a burning
house, a traveller who was shot by a highwayman and had a bullet in
his spine, and a builder who fell 60 feet while repairing the Chien Men
tower and was miraculously unhurt.

The police officers themselves provided clinical challenges, since
their enthusiasm put them in all kinds of danger. They were kicked,
beaten, stabbed, crushed by runaway mules and thrown from horses.
One suffered a skull fracture with amnesia and one developed an arte-
rial aneurysm from a bullet wound in his arm.

Another constable was nearly killed by a murderous trap not intended for him. A householder, who was fed up with being burgled,
set up a blunderbuss with a trip wire. The unlucky officer stepped on it
while doing his rounds and took the full blast on his legs. A tense situation arose: if the victim died of his wounds, the householder would
be condemned to death for taking the law into his own hands. Thomas
Stuckey performed a lengthy operation and removed 15 pieces of shot
from the policeman's legs before infection could get a grip. Happily
the officer was discharged fit for duty.

---

[3] See the Epilogue for details.

Another memorable case from this time involved a farmer called Fu. This time Ernest Peill was called and he found him helpless on his *kang*, too weak to move. Seven days earlier Mr Fu had asked a Chinese doctor to treat him for a sore throat. The doctor decided that a demon had taken up its abode in Fu's gullet and unless it was driven out, he would die. Radical treatment was prescribed. Two long needles were heated until they glowed and one was thrust transversely through the poor man's neck. The other was pushed behind his sternum for a distance of several inches.

From that moment Mr Fu was in agony, unable to eat or drink anything. Peill took one look and ordered a stretcher to get him to hospital. While a basket was being fetched, he did not lose the opportunity to tell the gaping crowd about Jesus and his love for all men and women. At the hospital he passed a gastric tube, rehydrated the patient and enabled wound healing to take place. Ten days later the man was sent home, well and swallowing normally.

Peill also operated on a young man with a minor eye problem who had foolishly allowed an old woman posing as an eye expert to insert needles into his eyeballs. (The Chinese faith in needling arose from their attachment to acupuncture.) His eyes were completely sealed up and his sight imperilled before he came to Peill's attention.

In another notable case the patient was a Buddhist priest from a village situated between Peking and Tientsin. He owned a temple and was known as 'Chang the Perfect', until his health broke down and he became less than perfect. When the doctors treated him successfully he became a believer and handed over his temple for Christian worship. The idols before which the villagers had prostrated themselves for generations were thrown out.

Cases like these made a big impression on local communities; ignorance and superstition wavered when confronted with effective scientific cures. The Imperial Court was no exception. Perhaps the most famous patient from this era was the younger brother of Empress Dowager Cixi, a middle-aged man of whom she was extremely fond. She ordered five court physicians to treat him, until she discovered that their prescriptions contradicted each other. One had the effect of raising body temperature and another of lowering it, and so on. Cixi was so angry that she had all five beaten and wrote her own prescription. That did not work either, so she sent her brother to the Lockhart Hospital, ordering the royal physicians to accompany him and report back all that the missionaries did.

A warm spirit of evangelism pervaded the hospital and the college. The doctors were powerful men of God and were delighted to find an open door for the gospel. Ernest Peill was one of three brothers who devoted their lives to China. He wrote, 'It is a great joy and privilege to be able to minister to the sick and suffering, but a still greater joy and privilege is that of being able to bring the good tidings of great joy to them in their sadness.'

The outpatient waiting room also served as a chapel and preaching went on every day from midday to 5 p.m. It followed a careful programme, covering the ministry of Jesus and the main points of Christian doctrine in the space of a month. In the wards a Chinese evangelist was constantly at work, teaching the catechism and giving out Bibles and tracts. The number of converts was small but the missionaries were not discouraged because every patient learned something of the gospel each time he or she attended. Some kept returning long after they were discharged from medical care.

In 1910 a *Times* correspondent toured the main medical missions in China and found that the Union Medical College was 'one of the most admirable of these institutions'. Three lamas from the famous Yellow Temple in Peking were undergoing treatment. He wrote, 'When one remembers what a hotbed of fanatical obscurantism that great lamasery has always been, such a fact speaks volumes.'

\*\*\*

During these years, the chief eunuch Li Lianying continued to visit Tom at night. He took a lively interest in the progress of the college and the two men became friends. He also arranged an audience in the Summer Palace for Tom to thank the Empress Dowager for her patronage. The setting was superb, a great palace alongside the Jade Lake, overlooking a camel-backed bridge and a marble boat on which Cixi loved to picnic. Beyond was the backdrop of the pagoda-crowned Western Hills. Tom wrote:

As far as I know, I am the only missionary who was ever granted the privilege of standing in front of the Dragon Throne. The scene was one of oriental splendour and dignity . . . The Empress Dowager sat enthroned. She looked every inch a queen, and supported with a quiet and splendid dignity a position which a long line stretching back to the beginning of history – a line of over two hundred monarchs – had occupied before her.

On the left and significantly below her sat the unhappy Emperor Guangxu, the puppet monarch whom Cixi had displaced and who looked exceedingly bored. Princes and high officials kowtowed to the Empress Dowager, and a flock of beautifully dressed ladies-in-waiting stood around in 'trembling attendance'. As a foreigner Tom was not permitted to speak; he had to fix his eyes on the carpet while an official read his memorandum. It was a European carpet of hideous design and entirely wrong in a room where everything else was exquisitely oriental. Who put it there, he wondered, and why? Was it a snub to Western merchandise?

Throughout the audience Cixi never looked at him. That was no surprise; a few years earlier she would have been hidden behind a silk curtain. But it saddened Tom who loved to engage in one-to-one relationships. He longed to tell Cixi of his love for China and the Chinese people. In later life he wondered if the Christian conversion of the old virago might not have brought as much blessing to China as a dozen medical schools.

The Empress Dowager had recently discovered photography and she allowed him to be photographed standing beside her while she stayed seated.[4] He never saw her again. Her final days were dedicated to trying to reverse the course of politics in China and save her own skin. Late in the day she appeared to espouse the merits of a constitutional monarchy and tried to produce a constitution on British lines. A draft document with an elected parliament and a limited franchise was published in August 1908, two months before her death. If she had lived longer, things might have turned out differently.

\*\*\*

---

[4] See p. 199 regarding this vanishing photograph.

While Cixi laboured on a draft constitution, Tom and Grace were in England settling their boys into boarding school. Grace had done her best to educate them at home in Peking but they fell behind. When Edgar was eight, they sent him to Eltham College, a school for missionaries' children in south London. The twins were nine when they joined him.

Missionary parents dreaded these separations, which often lasted many years. Grace had protected her children from tropical diseases, food poisoning, sandstorms, floods, bandits and Boxers. She had been nursemaid, teacher and defender, with little female company and with her husband often absent for long periods. Her children were infinitely precious to her and she never realized how painful the parting would be. She would no longer need to protect them like a lioness, but the house in Peking would no longer seem a home.

Tom was no less devastated. In his diary he likened his emotions to Abraham's struggle to sacrifice Isaac. He confessed that he only found the strength to part with his sons because of the promises that God gave Abraham on account of his faith. 'This means, my Father, that Thou wilt make it up to my three boys.'[5]

When the couple arrived back in Shanghai in November 1908, they were met by the news of the simultaneous deaths of the Empress Dowager and the Emperor. It was a huge shock. Everyone was asking, 'Both of them – *in a day*. How can it be?'

The Empress Dowager had been sick for some time. She was 73 years old and exhausted by diarrhoea and fever and by the task of drafting a constitution. It was 'time to mount the Dragon' and she must put her affairs in order.

But in an extraordinary reversal it was the deposed Emperor Guangxu who died first, at the age of 37 in the Summer Palace where he lived as a prisoner. He had been in poor health for some time. His physician recorded spells of violent stomach-ache when his face

---

[5] Interestingly they were not compelled to send them home. In the 1880s the China Inland Mission founded a boarding school in Chefoo (modern Yantai) for missionary children up to the age of 18. Chefoo was a treaty port on the Shantung peninsula only 300 miles from Peking, but Tom probably objected to its curriculum. It segregated the students from the Chinese, did not teach them Mandarin and even forbade them to speak it. This was wholly counter to his thinking.

turned blue. For some reason these features (which are fairly non-specific) were thought to be consistent with arsenic poisoning.

Murder was suspected but who was the culprit? Several people, including Yuan Shikai (a powerful figure at court who became the first formal president of the republic), had a motive, but none more so than Empress Dowager Cixi herself. Guangxu's attitude towards Japan had created a political nightmare for her. Between 1902 and 1908 the spectre of direct Japanese intervention in China haunted Cixi. A Sino-Japanese union or a 'Greater East Asia' was openly discussed in two capitals. True, Japanese thinking and efficiency might have reinvigorated China, but they would come at an impossible cost. Cixi was wholly opposed to Japanese overtures, but Guangxu was wide open. If he survived Cixi, he would imperil the Manchu dynasty and the whole Qing Empire.

Cixi was in the habit of sending the Emperor his favourite dishes, and Favourite Eunuch Li Lianying supervised the delivery, so she had the opportunity as well as the motive to poison him. One hundred years after Guangxu's death, toxicological analysis of his hair and clothes showed levels of arsenic that were many times the normal. Its concentration in the hair roots suggests that he died of a massive dose administered shortly before death.

Within hours Cixi appointed her three-year-old great-nephew Puyi as successor and his father as regent. She also appointed the Emperor's widow as Empress Dowager in her place, thus keeping the occupancy of the Dragon Throne within her family.[6] On 15 November 1908, the day after the Emperor's death and Puyi's installation, Cixi herself died. The timing of the events and the poison are strongly suggestive of a final act of foul play.

\*\*\*

The double funeral was a grandiose affair which cost the equivalent of £9 million today. Li Lianying stumbled along in the procession,

---

[6] Puyi was the subject of Bernardo Bertolucci's 1987 film *The Last Emperor*. He abdicated in 1912 and became (as Guangxu might have done had he survived) a Japanese pawn, ruler of a puppet state in Manchuria. He died in 1967.

clutching his mistress's favourite Pekingese dog in his arms. Did he have a direct hand in the timing of the Emperor's death? Probably not. His life was barely worth a *cash* with both Guangxu and Cixi dead. After the funerals, everything changed at court and he vanished. Perhaps it was as well from Tom's point of view. The role of father confessor might have been dangerous. Only the gifts on his mantelpiece reminded him of a friendship which had been so significant.

As life returned to normal in Peking, Tom and Grace wondered what would happen to China. Tom felt great sadness for the Empress Dowager. He had prayed for her for years but he never saw a change of heart. When sending any of her subjects to be treated at the hospital, she insisted they did not listen to Christian teaching.

***

The competence of Tom's students was about to be tested. In 1911 Peking was confronted with the horror of a plague epidemic. The ancient world feared plague almost as much as cholera. In southern China, 'port plague' lurked constantly and when the interior opened up, it was spread by the paddle steamers up the rivers. An epidemic in 1894 killed 60,000 inhabitants of Canton in a few weeks; then it spread 45 miles downriver to Hong Kong and killed 40,000 more.

The pestilence of 1910–11 started in Manchuria, where the provincial government was struggling with a Wild West situation. Russian and Japanese adventurers had extorted concessions to build railways and trading posts and a fierce struggle for trade was going on. The provincial authority was weak and it was in no condition to deal with a major epidemic.

Bubonic plague had long existed among the local marmots, a kind of large ground squirrel which harboured infected fleas. It was hunted for its fur which could be dyed to mimic sable and mink. Infected animals spread bubonic plague, but the epidemic that developed in 1910 was the pneumonic type which passes by droplet spread from person to person. It ran like wildfire through the settlements along 3,000 miles of railways. In 1910 there was no effective treatment for plague and the standard response was forced quarantine. In Manchuria this meant rounding up contacts at gunpoint and locking them in a railway wagon. If one person was infected, all were dead by the time the doors were opened three days later. At least 60,000 people died, with one known survivor.

As the epidemic spread south to Harbin, the Imperial Government dithered. It requested help from the Union Medical College and elsewhere, but it was too late to halt the advance of the disease. Several foreign doctors and students died in Harbin and the plague spread to Mukden before crossing the Gulf of Bohai. From there it threatened Peking.

The Union Medical College was appointed as a distribution centre for vaccines and ordered to prepare disinfectants and apparatus. By now the disease had reached Tientsin, 70 miles away. Two of the college's graduates and 13 senior students volunteered for duty there. The college report for 1910–11 states:

> A few days later a man was brought to our hospital [the Lockhart] in the evening, and died the next day at noon. The symptoms were very suspicious, and after a microscopic examination of the blood, our doctors were able to demonstrate the presence of the plague bacillus.

The authorities still prevaricated, but the UMC laboratory report forced them to close the source of infection, an inn in the South City, and to isolate all contacts. Peking was divided into sectors and inspectors were appointed. Every death was investigated and nobody could purchase a coffin without a safety certificate. Ten students from the Union Medical College supervised the work, which included compulsory house-to-house inspections. Within three weeks the plague was effectively stamped out. The college report ended, 'It is not too much to say that the work done by the college saved Peking from being handed over to the ravages of this dread pestilence in its most virulent form.'

Two of its senior students died, one of them 'a man of most beautiful Christian character'. The deaths drew the students together and several gave their lives to Jesus. The Imperial Government bestowed honours on the staff.

After the epidemic subsided, the official attitude towards Western medicine and scientific investigation changed. Plague hospitals were built and public health measures were introduced to major cities. The custom of four thousand years was re-examined. Post-mortem examinations had been permitted during the epidemic and an international conference in Mukden confirmed how important they had been. In November 1913 the new republic legalized them and anatomical dissections in general. These concessions helped to change public attitudes.

When the body of a criminal was publicly dissected at Kiangsu Medical College in Soochow, 65 VIPs attended. The event was considered so momentous that the guests and the deceased were photographed together in a scene reminiscent of Rembrandt's painting *The Anatomy Lesson of Dr Nicholaes Tulp*.

The following year another law allowed medical schools a quota of unclaimed bodies of executed convicts; the UMC was among the first to apply for its quota of three. The arrangement was not ideal because the bodies were often beheaded; in one city the military

*Graduation class at Union Medical College in mortar boards and Geneva gowns. April 1911 saw the birth of the first generation of Western-trained doctors in China*
Cochrane Family Collection

governor obligingly offered to have them strangled instead. Other medical schools were less quick to respond; they had never enjoyed the benefits of a mortuary or a post-mortem room and they had no money to build them anyway.

In 1915 a government directive laid down the standards required for degrees in medicine, pharmacy and veterinary science. It made no mention of traditional Chinese healing and gave official recognition to Western medicine. The Union Medical College curriculum became the blueprint for a coming generation of government-run medical schools. Tom's college could not have received a higher seal of approval.

# 15

## The Rockefeller succession

*Tom Cochrane in academic robes*
Author's collection

The fact that after only nine years of existence the Union Medical College passed out of the hands of the missionaries might be regarded as failure. But Tom Cochrane did not think so. As a boy I never thought to ask him about it, but he would probably have quoted the book of Proverbs 16.9: 'A man's heart deviseth his way: but the LORD directeth his steps.' In other words, it is God who has the last word in the end.

To understand the situation, one must know the background. On 10 October 1911 a bomb exploded in the capital of Hubei province, signalling the start of a revolution and the proclamation of a republic.

After 2,000 years of imperial rule, everything went into the melting pot: politics, religion, classes, education, foreign relations and the economy.

In later years Tom likened the hasty way in which a republic replaced the empire to the hideous carpet in the audience hall in the palace. 'I wondered, and have often wondered, that the Chinese allowed the whole rich pageant to pass away with so much unconcern. They and the world are the poorer.' He thought that a constitutional monarchy might have preserved China's historic past and bound the empire together in 'a progressive march'. But it was wishful thinking; there had been too much oppression and bloodshed. The break was swift and complete.

On the other side of the Pacific Ocean, the United States Congress welcomed the republic, probably relieved that it did not need to apologize too much for America's involvement in China. The USA had not pursued its interests as aggressively as the other Great Powers and laid no claim to Chinese territory. After the uprising, Congress returned its share of the Boxer Indemnity to the Chinese government for its educational programme.

The Americans saw the new republic as a bulwark against the growing ambitions of Japan. They were committed to strengthening it, to sharing their achievements in science and technology and, one need hardly add, to taking advantage of the vast markets that were opening up.

What of the spiritual welfare of China's millions? As the twentieth century advanced, evangelical Christians in America and Britain placed less emphasis on converting the heathen. They turned towards building schools and hospitals in order to improve education and health. Regarding health, American compassion was mixed with self-interest. Plague from Chinese ports crossed the Pacific and infected American cities. San Francisco suffered an epidemic that lasted from 1900 to 1904.

In 1914 the European nations became embroiled in a conflict that would bankrupt them and change the world for ever. The British Empire was threatened and had to be defended. Sea travel to the Far East became difficult. As the Old World stepped back, the New World stepped forward. America's hour in China had arrived.

***

By now the medical college had 130 students. Those in the senior year took their final examinations in the spring of 1911. Sixteen out of 21 candidates were awarded the first medical degrees ever conferred by the Chinese government. The fact that more than half of the students from the original year did not complete the course gives an idea of the challenges which they faced. Not the least was finding the money for tuition and residence. A graduation photograph shows the young men posing self-consciously in mortar boards and gowns in front of their residence.

Tom was now Principal Emeritus. He continued to demonstrate anatomy and do some operating, but his thoughts were elsewhere. He was in his mid-forties and after 14 years as a missionary he was probably suffering from burnout.[1] For many years his frustration with the home boards of the missionary societies in China had been growing. Their members seemed to think solely in terms of planting churches with foreign money, staffing them with foreign preachers and running them on foreign lines. This, he concluded, was the result of a racist attitude, something which he detested. He wrote in his diary, 'The missionary who talks about "allowing the natives" to do this, or "forbidding them to do that", should be recalled at once!' More publicly he wrote, 'The question which the modern missionary asks is "How soon can I render myself unnecessary?"'

The words 'native' and 'indigenous' had become his battle cry. He pleaded constantly for 'native' Chinese churches that were self-supporting and would plant the seed of the gospel in indigenous soil. That, he argued, would automatically produce good works in education, medical services, and social services like care of the elderly. With a little hindsight the argument is obvious, but this was the heyday of the Edwardian era. The British Empire was at its zenith and a quarter of the globe was coloured red. Even the missionary societies were tainted by colonialism.

The year 1911 was a watershed for Tom. He returned to Scotland on a much needed furlough which, apart from his convalescence after the

---

[1] In 1921 William G. Lennox, an American neurologist who had served for three years at Union Medical College, published a statistical survey entitled *The Health of Missionary Families in China*. He found that a quarter of missionaries left the mission field because of 'neurasthenia', that is, nervous breakdown or burnout.

Boxer Uprising, was probably only his second visit since 1897. He persuaded his society to set up an advisory body called the China Council to coordinate all missionary work throughout China and he returned to Peking bubbling with ideas. As its secretary, he started to travel widely outside Peking, visiting mission stations of all kinds, observing their work and their needs. The result was the *Survey of the Missionary Occupation of China*, published in 1913. It was a comprehensive survey of every province and included the number of stations, the number of workers (foreign and Chinese), their congregations, their financial resources, their churches, chapels and dispensaries, and the educational programmes in their primary and middle schools. The survey also included geographical notes on towns, villages, climate, agriculture, population distribution, and so on. There was an accompanying atlas.

Nothing remotely like this had been attempted before; the Chinese government had never even undertaken a population census. For the first time Christians could see what had been achieved for the gospel across the Chinese Empire and the enormity of the task that lay ahead.

One major failing which it revealed was the duplication of work and the waste of resources by the missionary societies. Most of this resulted from ignorance and unwillingness to change. It was galling to Tom because the solution seemed self-evident and he made plea after plea for 'wise, economical and efficient plans that would eliminate waste'. Years later his son Robert wrote:

> He had a sense of frustration, because men of lesser stature saw not
> the widening horizons of which he was conscious. Many a time those
> who knew him would say, 'Thomas Cochrane is twenty years ahead of
> his time,' and how correct they were!

I suspect that by the time Tom was halfway through making his survey, he knew that he had done all he could in Peking. The challenges which the survey opened up were immense and would demand his undivided attention. A different and greater work on a global scale was beckoning and the strategist must take over from the pioneer. In 1912 the Cochranes said their farewells and sailed for home. Tom remained an honorary director of the London Missionary Society but his service in the field was over. Nor did he practise clinical medicine again.

Writing 40 years later, he confessed that he missed his patients. 'I counted among my friends the highest officials in the empire. The gratitude of my patients is among my sweetest memories.'

\*\*\*

*The Rockefellers, father and son, in 1915, the year in which the Union Medical College was bought by the Rockefeller Foundation*
American Press Association

The rest of the UMC story belongs to others, so I shall be brief. In Peking Tom had prayed – without a hint of self interest – to become 'a millionaire for the sake of China', but God had a better idea. At the right moment, on the outbreak of the Great War, the richest man in the world appeared. John D. Rockefeller Senior, the founder of the Standard Oil Company, was a Baptist who had long supported evangelists in Asia. In 1913 he and his son set up the Rockefeller Foundation, the world's first medical philanthropic foundation. Its mission was 'to promote the well-being of mankind throughout the world'.

The Rockefellers were in a hurry to start investing and one of their first actions was to send a fact-finding commission to China. A four-man party arrived in Peking in April 1914 and visited Union Medical

College before going on to inspect 17 medical schools and 97 hospitals from Manchuria to Manila. Its report contained over a hundred pages of facts and recommendations.

Like Tom's *Survey of the Missionary Occupation of China* it was an eye-opener and the picture it painted was not rosy. A tiny proportion of the population had access to modern medicine, almost entirely through missionary hospitals and mainly in the treaty ports. There were about 250 hospitals and they were staffed by barely 300 foreign doctors; in other words, few employed more than one doctor. Female physicians made up a quarter of the number.

The hospitals were chronically short of money. Pay was low, nurses were few, basic facilities like running water were lacking and many buildings were poorly adapted. A dozen medical schools had been established but they were training fewer than 400 medical students. That worked out to less than one doctor per million of the population. The three big killers – tuberculosis, syphilis and hookworm – continued unchecked; in Shanghai in 1906 one in four deaths was due to tuberculosis. Leprosy and smallpox were also serious problems in many provinces. There were no sanatoria, no mental health asylums, no public health programmes and no laboratories dedicated to controlling diseases.

In Peking the Rockefeller party found that the Union Medical College and the Lockhart Hospital were failing to keep up with the huge demands placed on them. There were still only five buildings on the Hatamen Street site and the hospital had no more than 90 beds, 60 for men and 30 for women, not nearly enough for the task.

The college was faltering. It was graduating only a handful of students and desperately needed money to fund bursaries, new chairs and a proper library. The commission decided that its teaching standards were below those of American colleges and wrote patronizingly of its 'creditable beginnings' and of the missionaries' lack of academic qualifications. Only 38 students had graduated so far, with another 138 in training.

Those problems were merely the tip of a gigantic iceberg. In the 1900s medicine had entered an age when heavy capital investment was imperative. Without the facilities which we now take for granted like X-ray departments, operating suites, autoclaves, pharmacies, modern laundries and clinical laboratories, neither medical care nor medical education could advance.[2]

At the same time the Union Medical College was an attractive proposition. Located in the capital, it was by far the best medical school in China and the only one recognized by the Imperial Government. It had an income of $47,000 in gold and a faculty of 14 foreign doctors. It already received considerable public money for its services, and its excellence in the plague epidemic of 1911 had been officially recognized.

After inspecting medical colleges up and down China, the Rockefeller commission came to its conclusion:

> The Union Medical College at Peking, while its organization is not wholly satisfactory, appears to be more firmly established and better supported than any other missionary institution in the country. It has the largest faculty and more students and graduates than any other. Some of the teachers from their records should be qualified for useful work as teachers of medicine and its new hospital should do a great deal to establish a high standard of hospital practice in China.

The college was thus singled out as the best place for the Rockefellers to start putting their millions. It was better to build on well-established foundations than to start from scratch. In a word, they should buy the place. Yes, there were weaknesses in its administration, but these could be remedied by incorporating it into Peking University.

The die was cast. A division called the China Medical Board was established to bring together American know-how and Rockefeller dollars and to conduct negotiations. Its officers were some of the most astute academics in the USA.

In the talks that followed there was no way to avoid distress to the missionaries. It was clear that the gospel would no longer be preached, though John Rockefeller Senior promised that staff would be selected from persons 'sympathetic with the missionary spirit and motive'. But the men of God feared that the yardstick would be academic merit.

---

[2] A hospital administrator once asked me, 'Which part of a hospital is the most essential to the whole?' As a doctor I suggested A&E or some other clinical department. His answer was the humble laundry. A malfunction there will close a hospital almost overnight.

They were right, and the spiritual atmosphere of the college gradually evaporated.[3]

Then there was the thorny matter of language. For years there had been a lively debate in educational circles on whether to teach science in Chinese or English. The China Medical Board wanted English in order to recruit the best teachers from the USA. They also argued that Chinese students needed to be able to read Western medical literature and to study abroad. Already the Rockefellers offered free scholarships in other subjects at American colleges to English-speaking Chinese.

The missionaries were incredulous. 'The foundation of language is *thought*,' they exclaimed. 'You can't teach a Chinese to think in English!' And it was unfair: students from poor families would have to spend three years learning a foreign language, while those from wealthy families were likely to speak it already.

It also seemed that the long years which the missionaries had spent painstakingly creating a glossary of medical terms and translating textbooks into Chinese were being thrown away. Why do this? Surely *all* teaching would be in Chinese sooner or later? In that matter too they would be proved right.

Back in London, Tom's opinion as the college's founder was sought and he wrestled long and hard with the American offer. Had he put himself and his family through such hardships and dangers for everything to end like this? Did God really want newcomers who did not have the same love for China as the missionaries to pick up the baton? He thought of the millions of dollars which the Rockefellers talked of spending and of the £40 with which he had set out in 1901. If only he had been given that kind of money.

Eventually he was reconciled to the change. To say he had no regrets would be wrong, but the dream of creating the finest medical school in China had stalled. The Rockefellers had deep pockets; they could refinance the college on a scale that no one else could contemplate and thereby ensure its future.

There was another important factor to consider. For years Tom had taught that missionaries represented a transitional phase in creating

---

[3] The first generation of academics were also very young. Dr Franklin McClean, the first director of the college, was a bachelor of only 30 when appointed.

an indigenous church; one day they would – they must – hand everything over to Chinese pastors and ministers. In the same way, medical missionaries were transitional because their work would sooner or later be absorbed in the country's own health services. He probably realized, too, that as medicine became more sophisticated, it would be identified more with science and technology and less with the healing art. It was time to bow out.

In spring 1915 he travelled to New York on behalf of the London Missionary Society to negotiate the details. In June the Rockefellers purchased the Union Medical College for $200,000. It was a pittance compared with what they were about to spend.

In July 1915 the China Medical Board assumed control. Students in the senior years being taught in Mandarin were allowed to finish their studies in Peking, but those in the junior years were packed off to a university 300 miles away in Shantung province. A premedical school was started for the sons of prosperous families who had a basic knowledge of English. Thus the language question was settled.

The board bought another ten acres on Hatamen Street and started a building boom. The cornerstone for a new medical college was laid in September 1917. The plans included separate buildings for pathology, bacteriology, chemistry, physiology, pharmacology and a nurse-training school. Fourteen main buildings and 55 residences and auxiliary buildings sprang up. Their flared roofs clad in green tiles rested on massive decorated beams and bright vermilion columns, with balustrades of white-veined marble. The design was typical of a Chinese palace and was intended to reassure a population who remained obstinately suspicious of all things foreign. Professor J. Z. Bowers, when writing a history of the Rockefeller era, titled his book *Western Medicine in a Chinese Palace*.

Rebuilding the hospital and the college (renamed the Peking Union Medical College) took six years, during which the clinical and academic staff grew to over a hundred, together with a large number of administrative, clerical and technical staff. In September 1921 an official opening was held, attended by 1,300 guests, including 325 medical missionaries. Tom Cochrane travelled from Vancouver in a steamship packed with doctors and scientists from Europe and America. Others came from all over the Far East. The ceremonies lasted for a week. It was the largest medical conference China had seen, with lectures and clinical demonstrations.

Some of the doctors present had toiled for years in the tropics and remembered the college opening in 1906. They were blown away. These facilities were far superior to those in their own medical schools back home. The library contained 10,000 books and hundreds of foreign journals. The modern kitchens made the conventional smoke-filled Chinese kitchen look like something from the Stone Age. A steam laundry washed 3,000 items a day in copper vats and the telephone exchange served 300 extensions. There were massive electricity generators (AC and DC) and machines to produce gas, oxygen, steam and nitrous oxide. All these were piped directly to wards and theatres. There was a modern sewage treatment system, machine shops for everything from woodwork to electroplating, and even an ice-making plant.

But to veteran China hands, the greatest marvel was something very simple. It was the water, crystal clear, purified and chilled, that gushed from chrome taps in every department. That was a world away from pans of muddy liquid collected from a stream which then needed sieving and boiling. Progress indeed.

The Rockefellers had spent nearly $8 million and they had only just begun. By 1951 the China Medical Board had invested $45 million in the college. Both are staggering sums when corrected for modern values.

Tom Cochrane had a good week. He was presented to the president of the Chinese Republic who listened with interest to the story of the college. He also met John Rockefeller Junior and thanked him. 'I told him my bones and my blood had gone into its foundation and that the China Medical Board had carried out its promises, both in spirit and in letter.' A White House physician told him that the US president Warren Harding was personally delighted that everything was 'an extension of the work begun by the missionaries'.

That evening Tom attended a dinner at the Grand Hotel for former students, more than half of whom had become missionaries. He told them that his dream had been fulfilled and quoted the book of Chronicles: 'the house to be built for the LORD must be exceedingly magnificent, famous and glorious throughout all countries' (1 Chronicles 22.5 NKJV).

\*\*\*

There is no disputing that over the next 20 years the Peking Union Medical College did excellent work in teaching and research, nor that it set a standard by which other colleges throughout the East were measured. It pioneered new treatments and vaccines and produced new drugs. It even found a way to manufacture ephedrine from a weed found growing alongside the Great Wall. All these achievements were part of the China Medical Board's wider commitment to China through grants, educational schemes, nutritional research, public health programmes, bursaries, travelling fellowships and professional ethics. The board also helped pioneer the training of nurses and paramedical disciplines, which were still in their infancy in China.

The fact remained that the college was less interested in medical students and patients than in creating an elite research centre for postgraduates. Its commitment was (in the words of one Rockefeller trustee) to 'backing brains'. The undergraduate curriculum was more demanding than any in America or Europe, but in 19 years it produced only 313 doctors, more than half of whom left China. Those who stayed were loath to abandon the advantages of the treaty ports for the interior. Tom's vision of a flood of graduates pouring into China's countryside to practise preventative as well as therapeutic medicine was no nearer.

The huge cost of the Peking Union Medical College had other adverse effects. The Rockefellers had planned to build other colleges, but this one gobbled up the budget. The Chinese Ministry of Education was not always happy about it. In the 1930s it pressed for papers to be published in Chinese, for more Chinese teachers, more instruction in Chinese, and for practical courses in bacteriology and public health.

In 1937 the Japanese invaded mainland China. The college continued teaching until the attack on Pearl Harbour, when the director was thrown into prison and the campus was occupied. In 1949 the Communists gained power and the missionary era ended; by 1952 every foreigner had been expelled from the country. The college was denounced for its American connections and all ties with the Rockefellers were severed. Its official records were destroyed in the Cultural Revolution (1966–76). Over the years, the hospital underwent various changes of name and at one time was known as the Anti-Imperialist Hospital.

The wheel of fortune takes strange turns. In the event it was not Christianity, the Rockefeller millions or modern science that redeemed the health of China. It was the political will of a Communist regime, enforced through harsh ideological discipline. In a few years it achieved more than all the emperors, missionaries, philanthropists, scientists and reformers put together. An army of 'barefoot doctors' was trained in basic hygiene, and it marched out to educate the nation, at gunpoint if necessary, village by village and street by street. The people were forced to cleanse their environment and to wage war on the myriads of vectors which allowed diseases to flourish: flies, mosquitoes, fleas, lice, ticks, bedbugs, worms, snails and animals. The same hard-line ideological approach was used to suppress the use of opium.

That being so, one is bound to ask the question: was Tom Cochrane's work a failure? To that I say a resounding *no*. He was not just a quiet man who never lost faith in God. The medical college was an important step in breaking down hostility towards the West. The Christian instruction of students, staff and patients had consequences which cannot be measured. In a pitiless society the college declared Jesus Christ's message of caring for the poor and the unwanted. The instruction 'Love thy neighbour as thyself' lies at the heart of the healing art. Without it, doctors and nurses are deprived of something profound.

As Tom himself put it, 'The knowledge that the name of Yeh-su stands for healing and education and kindness, and an intense and practical selfless concern for all the highest interests of the people of the country, is working like leaven everywhere.'

To put his work into a broader perspective, we must remember that the Union Medical College was just one seed sown by missionaries across the Chinese Empire. It takes its place alongside a great planting of schools, universities, orphanages, hospitals, dispensaries, bookshops, printing works, churches and chapels. Tom's silk-covered subscription list was titled *Ten Thousand Good Deeds Brought Together*, and across the empire there were many thousands of other such deeds.

China today, in the twenty-first century, is gripped by an inner thirst which cannot be quenched by a cocktail of egotism, materialism and digital technology. All the evidence says that the nation is stirring spiritually, and that a new harvest from that sowing is not far off.

\*\*\*

My last footnote. After more than a hundred years of wars, civil wars, rebellions and revolutions, the college planted by Tom Cochrane and continued by the Rockefellers still exists in Beijing. It has reverted to the name of the Peking Union Medical College. Now largely a collection of postgraduate institutes, it is an academic centre and Beijing's premier centre for treating foreigners. The China Academy of Medical Sciences operates from its campus.

*Part of the Peking Union Medical College today*
Photograph courtesy of Ivan Walsh

# Epilogue: After China

———•◆•———

Tom returned to England in 1912 with a reputation as a pioneer. For many years he was known as 'Cochrane of China', though he never served overseas again. People wondered if his best years were behind him, but they proved to have been a preparation for what lay ahead. He joined forces with two men whose thinking, like his own, was 20 years ahead of its time. One was Roland Allen (1868–1947), a former missionary to China. He was their theologian and his experiences led him to reassess radically the theology and the practice of mission. He wrote influential books with provoking titles like *Missionary Methods: St Paul's or Ours?* His views did not sit well with many home boards.

Sidney Clark (1862–1930) was a wealthy London clothier who had retired from business at the age of 45. His fortune sponsored the ministry of the three men. He also learned about world mission the hard way, tramping the roads of Asia and Africa with a pencil and notebook in his hand. In China he visited nearly 600 market towns and thousands of surrounding villages. He was appalled by the inefficiency and waste and declared, 'If I conducted my business the way the missionary societies conduct theirs, I should be bankrupt!' He probably first met Tom in Peking in 1906.

The trio shared a passion to improve mission and to spread the 'indigenous principles' of self-support, self-propagation and self-government which Tom had taught for so long. In 1920 Tom and Roland Allen published the *Survey of the Missionary Occupation of China as an Aid to Intelligent Co-operation in Foreign Mission*. It remained a standard reference book for many years. In 1924 they founded the Survey Application Trust which published other on-the-spot surveys, including a *World Survey of Leprosy* in 1928. These reports covered every mission field on earth and were designed not only to prevent duplication and waste but also to highlight areas where there was little or no missionary effort. The trust's publishing arm, the World Dominion Press, produced a stream of books and articles, including *World Dominion*, a quarterly which continuously reported on mission worldwide. Tom launched the *World Christian Handbook* in 1949, a precursor of *Operation World*. Five editions were published before 1967.

*Thomas Cochrane in later life*
Cochrane Family Collection

In 1931 Tom raised the funds to purchase the Mildmay Centre in Bethnal Green in east London. It was built by a Victorian clergyman to bring relief to the desperately deprived borough and had seen hard use by the YMCA during the Great War. A small hospital on the site treated sick missionaries and their families. (My tonsils were removed there by a missionary surgeon in 1944.) Today the hospital is a specialist centre for treating patients with complex HIV-related conditions.

At Mildmay Tom founded the Movement for World Evangelization which, with the World Dominion Trust and the International Fellowship for Worldwide Witness, formed the so-called Mildmay Movement. The conferences which he organized in the 1930s and 1940s inspired many to participate in mission activities. A spirit of evangelism radiated out from Mildmay.[1]

All three of Tom's sons became distinguished doctors. Edgar was a medical officer in the Colonial Office and led a successful campaign in the Aden Protectorate against tuberculosis, which claimed many lives there each year. As a schoolboy I visited Aden in 1950 and saw how the local leaders honoured him. He had announced his impending retirement, and in protest Jews, Arabs and Bedouins gathered on his doorstep and prepared to sacrifice two sheep. His wife Nan, who was a great animal lover, rescued the creatures and probably made pets of them. Edgar bowed to the pressure and postponed his retirement.

The older twin, Robert, went to India in 1924 as a Church of Scotland missionary. He later became principal and director of the Christian Medical College in Vellore and a world authority on leprosy, advising the World Health Organization and the British government. I knew him in London when I was a medical student in the 1960s and received much encouragement from him. The younger twin, called Thomas after his father, had a long and fruitful career as a consultant surgeon in the Dartford area of Kent.

The next generation of Cochranes continued the medical tradition. In the early 1950s no fewer than four of Tom's grandsons were medical students together at St Bartholomew's. A granddaughter trained there at the same time as a nurse. I suspect this is a record for any family (or medical school).

Grace Cochrane died in 1930 in Orpington. A few years later Tom married again, to my maternal grandmother Edith Ervine. He acquired six stepdaughters and over time a total of 11 stepgrandchildren

---

[1] Tom also helped to found the World Aviation Fellowship, a forerunner of the Mission Aviation Fellowship (MAF), which uses light aircraft to bring medical supplies and assistance to the most remote parts of the world. Murray Kendon, a Second World War pilot, had a vision for this work and in 1946 he met Tom, who helped him pursue it. He published an article by Kendon which triggered much interest in the flying world and led eventually to the formation of MAF.

who knew him as the Doc, Uncle Tom or simply as Grandpa. We held him in various mixtures of awe and affection. Grandmother and Tom kept a close eye on my own family during the Second World War, when my father served as an anaesthetist in the Royal Army Medical Corps. He was away for nearly five years in Malta, Egypt and Gaza, and much of the time we had no idea where he was. Some of my earliest memories are of staying with the elderly couple in the administrator's house at Mildmay. It was a place of wonder, furnished in oriental fashion with lacquered cabinets, hand-painted silk screens and decorative carpets. Tom had a sweet tooth and at lunch he ladled his sugar ration into a bowl of tomato soup. At the time I wondered if it was an ancient Chinese custom.

During the Blitz the Luftwaffe rained incendiary bombs on north London and we huddled in the basement of the Mildmay conference centre. One night the whole of the neighbourhood seemed to catch fire and buses exploded outside the gates, but the centre came through unscathed. Tom was unfazed by the racket. He had seen it all 40 years earlier.

In 1951 the London County Council needed land for housing and acquired Mildmay by compulsory purchase. Tom retired and seemed to slow down a bit. He often said that all his prayers in life had been answered, which seemed a tall order to me as a youngster. But he meant it; through his habit of 'listening prayers' he had learned to determine God's will for his life and to pursue only that. He encouraged me from an early age to do likewise and to be what he called 'a true Christian gentleman'.

In 1951 my family's fortunes were at a low ebb. My parents had divorced, my father had lung tuberculosis (he never worked again) and my mother was depressed. Of a sudden she emigrated to Australia, taking me with her. Things did not work out and we returned penniless and with my schooling disrupted. Tom wrote to the headmaster of Epsom College, a public school for the sons of doctors. Introducing himself as the founder of the premier medical school in China, and writing as one principal to another, he gave me a glowing recommendation. I doubt the headmaster ever had another letter like it. After setting me some exam papers, the college gave me a scholarship which covered my education for the next six years. My debt to it and to Tom is considerable.

In October 1953, with his health failing, he travelled from Pinner in Middlesex to Chelmsford in Kent to comfort an old lady who was newly bereaved. It was typical of a man whose life was dedicated to serving others. He died at Pinner that December, full of years and loved by many, including many who knew little of his achievements in China. At his funeral service, we sang Isaac Watts' great missionary hymn:

> Jesus shall reign where'er the sun
> Doth his successive journeys run;
> His kingdom spread from shore to shore,
> Till moons shall wax and wane no more.

# Appendix 1

# Empress Dowager Cixi (1835–1908)

Empress Dowager Cixi has had a very mixed press. Her name (pronounced *tseshee*) means 'auspicious and motherly', but her conduct never matched up to it.

Cixi was a remarkable individual and probably the most powerful woman in China's long history. That much cannot be denied. She lived in a misogynistic and male-dominated society in which she rose from modest beginnings to the top. She effectively occupied the throne for over 40 years, steering the Qing Empire through a succession of foreign incursions and wars, internal rebellions and other desperate crises.

She was born into the ruling Manchurian class in 1835 and at the age of 16 became an imperial concubine of the Third Rank. Though she lacked formal education, she was shrewd and lucky. In 1856 she bore the Xiamen Emperor a male heir. The boy's official mother, the Empress Zheng, was grateful and the two women became allies. When the emperor died in 1861, Cixi's child, Tongzhi, succeeded to the throne.

Confronted by a panel of hostile regents, the two women launched a daring coup which would have earned them death by a thousand cuts if it had failed. By Qing standards it was relatively bloodless; only two out of eight regents were killed. Cixi was recognized as a second empress dowager and the women divided the reins of power. They held joint audiences behind a silk screen that separated them from their officials. Everything was done in the name of the child-emperor.

After the Taiping Rebellion, China enjoyed a period of relative peace and economic recovery. The closed-door policy on trade was reversed and the interior of the country opened up. Robert Hart was appointed Inspector-General of the Imperial Customs Service, with spectacular results. A debate on modernization began. The imperial fleet was equipped with Western gunboats and ordnance. The centuries-old seclusion of China ended as the government sent missions and students abroad to study the West. In all these matters Cixi's role is still debated. It is unclear to what degree she was an initiator and reformer as opposed to a reluctant rubber-stamper.

In 1872 the young Emperor Tongzhi married and acceded to the throne. Despite the urging of his two mothers, he was far more interested in sex than politics and shirked his responsibilities. In 1874 he died of smallpox and his wife starved herself to death as a mark of respect. It was rumoured that Cixi had the couple murdered to regain power, but evidence is lacking.

Cixi could only exercise power by establishing a regency and she lost no time in nominating another youngster to the throne, her three-year-old nephew Guangxu. The regency lasted from 1875 to 1889. The reforms continued: ambassadors were appointed to Western capitals, more officials were sent abroad to study Western institutions, and a start was made on modernizing the Civil Service examinations. The Chinese Post Office was inaugurated in 1878. The telegraph system, coal mining and electricity production were birthed, but railways remained controversial. The modernization of the navy was completed, giving China for a brief time the most powerful navy in Asia.

Cixi's collaborator, Empress Zheng, died in 1881 aged only 43. Rumour had it that Cixi sent her poisoned cakes, but the court medical records suggest that she had already suffered three strokes. She died after two days in a coma, which fits better with a stroke.

Emperor Guangxu was thrifty and cautious, a model Confucian. He cared for his subjects in principle but he was not very practical. In 1886 he turned 15 and should have succeeded to the throne, but Cixi found a way to buy time. She persuaded his father to force him to petition her to continue as regent. Guangxu became increasingly bitter towards Cixi, especially since she insisted that he address her bizarrely as 'My Royal Father' and selected a bride whom he detested.

When Guangxu finally acceded in 1889, Cixi retired to the Summer Palace, a collection of palaces, temples and pavilions set in beautiful parklands outside Peking. An Anglo-French punitive expedition had looted and burned much of the Yuanmingyuan, or Old Summer Palace complex, in 1860. Now in her sixtieth year, Cixi restored one palace, the Yiheyuan, for her own use. This led to the charge of siphoning off navy funds and causing China's disastrous naval defeat in 1894. In fact the sums were modest (she embezzled interest, not capital) and research suggests that it had no significant effect on China's war effort.

At the Yiheyuan Cixi lived surrounded by her ladies-in-waiting, her eunuchs and her pets. Her days revolved around painting, boating and operatic performances. Guangxu meanwhile was open to outside overtures, including those of Japan, which appalled Cixi. At the same time he was also open to the West, which delighted some Chinese who believed an alliance with the Christian nations was the only way to save China. For a time the question of adopting Protestantism as the national religion was discussed at court and the demand for Bibles and religious books was so great that the Chinese printing houses could not meet it.[1]

Guanxu was kept ignorant about the military threat from Japan and China's relative weakness until 1894, when Japan launched a devastating war of expansion in Korea. It ended with China accepting a treaty so humiliating that it threatened to bring the Qing Empire to an end. Cixi was furious with Guangxu for accepting the terms.

In 1898 Guangxu finally took action, though not of a kind which Cixi necessarily approved. He dismissed his ultra-conservative tutor, who had advised for years against reforms, and introduced new advisers, including the reformer Kang Youwei. During the so-called 'Hundred Days' they drew up a series of paper reforms covering politics, education, the Civil Service examinations, agriculture and commerce. If introduced they might have made Guangxu the head of a constitutional government with real powers.

The uneasy relationship between nephew and aunt ended abruptly when Cixi discovered that Guangxu was implicated in a plot against

---

[1] Tom's journal mentions a Christian bookshop near the Peking headquarters of the London Missionary Society where in the early 1900s the imprisoned Emperor sent his eunuchs to buy books. When a group of Chinese women presented the Empress Dowager with a New Testament, the Emperor sent out for a Bible. Tom presented him with two books by the evangelical Timothy Richard, *The History of the Nineteenth Century* and *Essays of Our Times*. None of this would have been pleasing to Cixi.

her life. (To avoid a dynastic crisis, the matter was hushed up and only came to light in the 1980s in government archives.) Cixi moved swiftly; she snatched back power and placed Guangxu under house arrest, in which he spent the rest of his miserable life. When the pair fled Peking during the Siege of the Legations in August 1900, she ordered his favourite concubine to be thrown down a well.

The rest of Cixi's story is told in the narrative. During 1905–8 she was forced to resurrect the political reforms mooted by her opponents in 1898, but it was too little and too late. If she had been able to introduce a constitutional democracy, her legacy might have been different.

As I have indicated, history has not been kind towards Cixi as the 'auspicious and motherly'. Ruthless, murderous, lascivious, greedy and tyrannical are descriptions more often used. In China the process of demonization started before her death. Her harshest critic was Kang Youwei, who after the 1898 assassination plot fled to Japan and became one of a long bitter line of enemies and critics. Another source close to her was Der Ling, a lady-in-waiting and self-styled princess. In *The Old Buddha* she wrote of Cixi's hatred for all foreigners who took it on themselves to criticize her government. Her special anger was reserved for the missionaries; she endorsed the slanders about experiments on children and the use of pulverized eyes as medicines.

Der Ling claimed to recall Cixi's exact words. For example:

> Our country was a civilized country while the people in so-called civilized countries were still swinging by their tails from trees. Yet those same countries have the audacity to send missionaries to us to teach us religion and civilization! Suppose I were to flood foreign countries with Buddhist priests! . . . The foreigners are the curse of China today and I would be the happiest woman in the world if there were some way to rid China of them forever.

In the West these accounts, together with her treacherous conduct during the Boxer Uprising and her anti-reform stance, have shaped Cixi's reputation. A forger and fantasist called Edmund Backhouse, who lived in Peking, wrote two influential books which fuelled the fire. *China under the Empress Dowager* (1910) was allegedly based on the diary of a court official, but it was a forgery which the British historian Hugh Trevor-Roper unmasked four decades later. Backhouse's own memoirs (titled *Manchurian Decadence*) were full of pornographic allegations about Cixi's private life. He himself claimed to have had an affair with her (and with others, including Lord Rosebery, Oscar Wilde and an Ottoman princess).

In the 1950s Communist polemicists accused Cixi of fatally weakening the empire and allowing it to fall under Western influences. But in recent years, as China has sought to redefine its past, there has been a change. Cixi has been refashioned as a patriot who fought fiercely to protect China's sovereignty against the arrogance and encroachment of the imperialist nations.

The Chinese writer Jung Chang has also presented Cixi in a favourable light, as a significant political reformer, innovator and feminist. Her biography draws upon newly available court records, correspondence, diaries and eyewitness accounts.[2] But her conclusions have been rebutted by many historians, who argue that Chang (who is not a professional historian) has misinterpreted the sources and substituted one stereotype for another. Part of the story is that during the disastrous Taiping Rebellion, decentralization became essential to save the empire. Power drained steadily from the monarchy to powerful provincial governors and commanders on the spot, and the flow was never reversed. It was they who kept the monarchy afloat by initiating reforms, controlling the economy, deciding foreign policy and preventing the Boxer Uprising from developing into a full-scale war. According to this view, the Dragon Throne had become irrelevant to China's future long before Cixi's death in 1908.

Tom Cochrane would have known nothing about these great economic and geopolitical shifts and he never engaged in the debates that raged around the Empress Dowager. He saw her only as a benevolent despot, his benefactor and China's potential redeemer.

---

[2] *Empress Dowager Cixi: The Concubine Who Launched Modern China* (2013), Jonathan Cape, London.

# Appendix 2

# *Opium – the foreign smoke*

———

Like the African slave trade, the nineteenth-century opium trade in China was a monumental crime perpetrated by Westerners who insisted their behaviour was ethically defensible. They grew rich financially but became morally bankrupt. In the process the lives of millions of victims were ruined by their addiction. The main facts about the opium trade are well known, but the argument about who was responsible for it continues. I shall focus on the medical aspects, which are what concerned Tom Cochrane. They are often dismissed by liberal historians who claim the harm done by opium has been exaggerated.

The Chinese had grown poppy crops for generations before the Westerners arrived. They used opium in much the same way as our Victorian forebears, as an analgesic, a sedative and occasionally for pleasure. Any other usage was regarded as *tsui*, a sin, and the first decrees regulating poppy growing were promulgated in 1729.

At that time opium was mixed with tobacco and smoked in a short pipe. It is calculated that the smoker inhaled 0.2 per cent morphine by volume. In the mid-eighteenth century long-stemmed pipes were introduced and an opium paste introduced; it delivered 9 to 10 per cent morphine. And the Indian opium which the British brought to the table was of very high quality.

Britain's participation in the trade began because of that nation's love affair with tea. By 1750 British merchants were paying Chinese merchants a fortune in silver bullion for tea and luxury goods like silk and porcelain, while the Chinese disdained British exports.[1] The

---

[1] Between 1710 and 1759 Britain spent £26 million in silver bullion on Chinese goods, while the Chinese spent only £9 million on British products. The situation was further complicated because the Chinese would only accept payment in Spanish silver dollars.

opportunity to do something about the imbalance arose when Britain annexed Bengal in eastern India, where the poppy grew well. In 1782 Warren Hastings, the first governor-general of India, sent a small shipment of opium to China. The first auctions were a flop, which suggests that consumption was low and addicts few. But after a few years Indian opium caught on like wildfire. Selling to the Chinese brought several benefits. It redressed the balance of trade, it produced taxes for the British government and it brought wealth to India.

The truth is that Britain's presence in India was the driver for the British opium trade. India was 'the Jewel in the Crown', Britain's most prized possession, and after the Royal Titles Act of 1877 the reason that Victoria was an empress. But it was expensive to administer and defend.

Opium did great harm to India too. The princes and nabobs grew wealthy but the poor got poorer. Millions of addicts were created, a fact which the British administration ignored. A quarter of world trade had once originated in India but opium changed that. Thousands of growers shifted from cereals to quick cash crops, thereby creating food shortages. Many indentured labourers left the country, mainly from the poppy-growing areas. Pretty soon 17 to 20 per cent of Indian revenues came from the sale of opium. If you add in the shipping fleet, the factories and the other auxiliary industries, it is clear that this 'commodity' effectively financed British rule.

China was simply a market to be exploited, and those who profited were unconcerned for the consequences. In 1833 the East India Company lost its trade monopoly and the opium market exploded. The Chinese government repeatedly tried to control the trade and was ignored. When, in an act reminiscent of the Boston Tea Party, it retaliated by seizing and burning opium cargoes from India, Britain was outraged and called in the Royal Navy. The country successfully fought two 'opium wars' in 1839–42 and 1858–60 to protect 'free trade'.

War with China had been inevitable, so long as the West insisted on opening up China's markets and the Manchu emperors resisted. In that sense opium was only a trigger, and at least one historian has suggested that the Opium Wars should be called 'the Wars for Diplomatic Recognition'. But that in no way excuses the iniquity of some British actions.

After the Indian Mutiny in 1857, power passed from the East India Company to the India Office and a viceroy in Calcutta. The Chinese might have hoped for better treatment and a curb on the opium trade, but the Raj's interests came first. Britain began a period of intense capital investment in Indian railways, roads, ports, telegraphs and irrigation systems, which had to be paid for. With other revenues low, the Indian economy remained heavily dependent on opium. Between 1860 and 1900 the value of opium imports into China rose from £4.5 million to £9.5 million.

But in Britain consciences were stirring. In 1874 Evangelicals and Quakers founded the Society for the Abolition of the Opium Trade and repeatedly brought motions before the Commons. In 1891 Sir Joseph Pease appealed passionately to the MPs:

> In this House we have prayers read every day, and we pray that God's Kingdom will come upon earth. If we go on with this opium trade, we are not spreading God's Kingdom; we are spreading the kingdom of the devil.

In 1893 Parliament set up a Royal Commission which sat for nearly two years and produced a report 2,500 pages long. It pushed abolition off the parliamentary agenda for over a decade.

It was not that the commissioners were ignorant or venal. They were honourable men who travelled to Calcutta to take evidence from over 700 witnesses and they worked according to parliamentary rules. But their brief had been subtly altered. The Commission became an enquiry into India as a purveyor of opium, not an examination of China as a force-fed victim. (The commissioners did not even visit China.)

The British administrators in India ensured that the hearings were a whitewash. On the critical point, the health effects of opium, the Commission's report stated:

> The gloomy descriptions presented to British audiences of extensive moral and physical degradation by opium, have not been accepted by the witnesses representing the people of India, nor by those most responsible for the government of the country.

One has to ask: were there really such differences between opium addicts in India and China? If so, there may be explanations. As I have observed, in China it was smoked and often cut with tobacco, which made it more addictive. In India it was *eaten* or dissolved in bowls of water. There were probably higher standards of health and nutrition in India. Dosages, frequency of the habit and the use of alcohol may have been lower in India. But the likeliest explanation is that the Commission's witnesses came from the upper ranks of Anglo-Indian society and they rarely saw the effects of the drug. As soon as a servant or a clerk became inefficient, he or she was sacked.

Doctors in India had no convincing evidence against opium simply because none had been collected; the royal commissioners were not medical men and all they heard were arguments unsupported by statistics. The *Lancet* was unimpressed by the medical evidence.

However, when the report was read in China the medical missionaries were outraged. They saw the ravages of opium on a daily basis. In Soochow a group came together and formed an Anti-Opium League. They sent a questionnaire to every foreign-trained doctor in the land and received over 100 responses, mostly from missionaries with an average of nine years' service. The results were collated by Dr William Park of Soochow Hospital and published in 1899 as *Opinions of Over 100 Physicians on the Use of Opium in China*. Its arguments are infinitely more cogent than anything in the Royal Commission report.

The survey detailed the physical, financial, moral and spiritual ruin caused by opium to the Chinese people. It describes the poverty, despair, suicide and crime. It describes families being broken up, children sold into slavery, wives sold into prostitution and brides being forced to share in the debauchery of their in-laws. Here are some individual conclusions by missionary doctors:[2]

> The evils arising from the abuse of opium in China cannot be overstated. It is sucking the life and energy out of this great nation.

> No language on earth contains words strong enough to describe the evils of opium smoking in China.

---

[2] This sample of opinions came from Dr Dugald Christie in Harbin, Manchuria; Dr William Park in Soochow; Dr V. P. Suvoong in Shanghai; Dr H. T. Whitney in Foochow; and Dr Robert Beebe in Nanking.

Opium is a moral poison and thereby largely responsible for the decay of this great empire.

[Opium addiction] practically shuts the door to the attainment of spiritual life.

My nearest neighbour . . . one by one sold his three children to gratify his habit. At last he sold his wife, quit his desolate house of reeds and wandered a vagabond and thief to prey upon the body politic.

But by 1899 the situation was beyond the control of the British Parliament because poppy cultivation in China itself had soared and overtaken imports from India. Farmers, carters, merchants, smugglers and officials relied on it for their living, and provincial governors for their taxes. In some provinces opium was used as currency. The Imperial Government repeatedly banned the planting of new crops but without effect. By 1906 China, which had once been the dumping ground for foreign opium, was producing nearly 35,000 metric tons, approximately 85 per cent of world production.

The following year Britain signed a treaty agreeing to eliminate all its opium exports to China within ten years and the Chinese government agreed to suppress domestic production. It failed, and in the turmoil that followed the fall of the empire, the market continued. Then in the 1950s the Communist Party presented the opium problem as a political challenge, a class struggle by the proletariat against their bourgeois oppressors. It was finally scotched by education, propaganda and the harsh punishment of the 'enemies of the people'.

# Appendix 3

## Imperial eunuchs

Eunuchs were employed in China for at least two millennia. They served the emperors of many dynasties and often played a part in their rise and fall. Their heyday was during the Ming dynasty in the early seventeenth century, when up to 100,000 lived in the Forbidden City. By 1900 approximately 2,000 remained. Much of our information comes from George Stent, an Englishman who served in the Indian Mutiny before he became a customs officer in China. In 1877 he published an essay about the eunuch system which he called 'a horrible mutilation of one sex to keep the other pure'. The gory details of castration surgery are all there.

Important differences existed between eunuchs in China and in other countries. In the latter, prisoners, rebels and troublemakers who offended their rulers were neutered as a punishment. Eunuchs were sold as slaves in the slave markets of the Middle East and North Africa. In China castration was voluntary. Why on earth did boys and young men make this choice? At least one son was needed to maintain ancestor worship, so only boys from desperate families with more than one son took this path. It was a way to avoid the whole family starving and to achieve a degree of security.

In the Middle East any rich individual could own eunuchs, but in China it was an imperial right. The Emperor maintained thousands, and other members of his family had a handful. The theory was that because eunuchs had no natural heirs, they would not be greedy for power or wealth. (In practice some served selflessly while others, like Li Lianying, did not.) They looked after the Emperor from his childhood and taught him everything. They were at his side day and night, caring for him in sickness and in health, enjoying a warm relationship. They brought the concubine of his choice to his chamber at night and kept a record of the visits for the happy day when she became pregnant.

They also controlled access to his presence. They could keep even members of the imperial family away until a bribe passed hands. Thus the word 'eunuch' became a byword for greed and duplicity. The people blamed them for all manner of evils. They likened them to termites which undermined buildings and sent them toppling.

In other countries eunuchs were principally 'guardians of the bed' (a literal translation of the Greek word). In Peking, however, they staffed 48 different service departments in the Forbidden City. They were gardeners, water carriers, messengers, watchmen, sedan-chair bearers and armourers. They looked after the wardrobes, the treasures, the food and the supplies. Three hundred actors, musicians and singers provided the court with entertainment. They were also cooks, butlers, scullions, chamber 'maids', clerks and much more.

The rationale for the system was that the Emperor was the agent of the Supreme God. By the late nineteenth century, much of his divinity had evaporated, but he kept himself remote from his subjects. It was essential that they did not see him as a mere man, and no commoner could enter the Forbidden City, a complex of palaces, pagodas and temples. The Celestial Palace was even more tightly sealed off. Here lived the Emperor with his harem and no man set foot, only eunuchs.

By 1900, educated Chinese had reached the conclusion that the eunuch system was an anachronism. The Great Powers did not have eunuchs, but only weak countries like Turkey. The knifers performed fewer and fewer castrations, and after the overthrow of the monarchy there was no call for them. When they were expelled from the Forbidden City in 1923, a few score half-starved individuals were thrown weeping on to the streets.

# Bibliography

Tom Cochrane intended to write an account of his time in China. Among his papers are outlines for a book, some of which have been annotated by another hand, probably Roland Allen's. The autobiography never materialized, but a number of articles did. The best ones he wrote for *The Christian Herald and Signs of Our Times* when he was in his eighties.

By then he struggled to remember the events of 50 or 60 years earlier and regretted that he had not kept better records. His personal notes do not always line up with his articles. An example is the young woman in labour described in Chapter 2. In one version Tom saved the baby as well as the mother; in others the baby was stillborn. This kind of discrepancy, though not critical, is a challenge for the biographer. I have met it by using what seems the more likely version. In the example quoted, there is no discredit to Tom, who probably confused two cases. He would have saved and lost many babies in China, where the infant mortality rate was four or five times greater than in Britain.

When he died, his papers were sorted and some were discarded. My mother claimed that they included a photograph taken during his audience with Cixi in 1906, showing the Empress Dowager seated and Tom in morning dress. She hunted high and low but never found it. If such a photograph existed, it would be unique. By 1906 Cixi had softened sufficiently to be photographed with the wives of diplomats, but missionaries were a different matter. If it turns up in somebody's album, I would give many *cash* to have a copy.

The Internet is a treasure trove of primary sources which have long been out of print and would otherwise collect dust in archives. Several works referenced below have been generously placed on the Internet.

They are marked with an asterisk, for the reader to hunt out and joyfully download.

Aitchison, G. M. (1983), *The Doctor and the Dragon*. Pickering & Inglis, Basingstoke.

Allen, H. J. B. (1995), *Roland Allen, Pioneer, Priest and Prophet*. Forward Movement Publications, Cincinnati.

Annual Reports of the Free Healing Hospital, Peking (1896, 1898). Tientsin Press, China.

Annual Reports of the North China Missions to the London Missionary Society (1891–1901). London.

Annual Reports of the Rockefeller Commission (1913–14, 1915, 1916 and 1917). New York.*

Annual Reports of the Society for the Diffusion of Christian and General Knowledge among the Chinese (1898, 1900). Printed by the *Shanghai Mercury*, China.

Annual Reports of the Union Medical College, Peking (1910, 1911, 1914). Tientsin Press, China.

Barmé, G. R. (2008), *The Forbidden City*. Profile Books, London.

Bickers, R. (2012), *The Scramble for China*. Penguin Books, London.

Bowers, J. Z. (1970), *Western Medicine in a Chinese Palace: Peking Union Medical College 1917–1951*. Josiah Macy Jr Foundation, New York.

Broomhall, M. (1901), *Martyred Missionaries of the China Inland Mission, with a Record of the Perils & Sufferings of Some Who Escaped*. Morgan & Scott, London.*

Brown S. (1985), *Heralds of Health*. Christian Medical Fellowship, London.

Chang, J. (2013), *Empress Dowager Cixi: The Concubine Who Launched Modern China*. Jonathan Cape, London.

China Medical Commission of the Rockefeller Foundation (1914), *Medicine in China*. New York.

Cochrane, M. G. (2018), *The Edge of the Cliff*. Eli Press, Bishop Auckland, Co. Durham.

Cochrane T. J. (various dates), *The Healing of a Nation*. Uncompleted manuscript. Also letters, day books and reports.

Cochrane, T. J. (1903), *Ten Thousand Good Deeds Brought Together*. Peking.

Cochrane, T. J. (1913), *Survey of the Missionary Occupation of China*. Christian Literature Society for China, Shanghai.

Cochrane, T. J. (1951–2), *The Christian Herald and Signs of Our Times* (articles), London.

Der Ling (1929), *The Old Buddha*. Dodd, Mead & Co., New York.

Dudgeon, J. (1877), *The Diseases of China*. Reprinted from the *Glasgow Medical Journal*.

Edwards, E. H. (1901), *The Reign of Terror in the Western Hills, or Stories of the Persecution of Chinese Christians in Shansi 1900*. Printed by the *Shanghai Mercury*, China.*

Fleming, P. (1959), *The Siege at Peking*. Rupert Hart-Davis, London.

French, F. (1956), *Thomas Cochrane, Pioneer and Missionary Statesman*. Hodder & Stoughton, London.

Gilmour, J. (1882), *Among the Mongols*. Reprinted in 2010 by Nabu Press, USA.*

Glover, A. (1904), *A Thousand Miles of Miracles in China*. Hodder & Stoughton, London.*

Goodall, N. (1954), *A History of the London Missionary Society, 1895–1945*. Oxford University Press, London.

Hanes, W. T., and Sanello, F. (2003), *The Opium Wars*. Robson Books, London.

Headland, I. (1909), *Court Life in China: The Capital, Its Officials and People*. F. H. Revell, New York.

Horn, J. S. (1969), *Away with All Pests: An English Surgeon in People's China*. Monthly Review Press, New York and London.

Incoming Correspondence of the London Missionary Society (1890s and 1900s). London.

Larson, F. A. (1930), *Larson, Duke of Mongolia*. Little, Brown and Company, Boston.*

Lennox, William G. (1921), *The Health of Missionary Families in China: A Statistical Study*. University of Denver, Colorado.*

Lewis, C. (1936), *Sagittarius Arising*. Penguin Books, London.

Lovett, R. (1899), *The History of the London Medical Society, 1795–1895*. Henry Frowde, London.

Lutz, J. G. (1971), *China and the Christian Colleges, 1850–1950*. Cornell University Press, Ithaca, New York.

McCasland, E. (2001), *Eric Liddell, Pure Gold*. Discovery House Publishers, Grand Rapids, Michigan.*

Mitamura, T. (1970), *Chinese Eunuchs: The Structure of Intimate Politics*. Charles E. Tuttle Co., Rutland, Vermont.

Park, W. H., ed. (1899), *Opinions of Over 100 Physicians on the Use of Opium in China*. American Presbyterian Mission Press, Shanghai.*

Royal Opium Commission (1895), *First Report of the Royal Commission on Opium*, Eyre & Spottiswoode for Her Majesty's Stationery Office, London.*

Spence, J. D. (1982), *The Gate of Heavenly Peace: The Chinese and Their Revolution, 1895–1980*. Penguin Books, London.

Stent, G. C. (1877), 'Chinese Eunuchs'. *Journal of the North China Branch of the Royal Asiatic Society*, No. 11, Shanghai.

Taylor, H. (1965), *Biography of James Hudson Taylor*. Christian Medical Fellowship, London.

# *Index*